MW01676323

A Theological Toolbox for Women

Reflective *Faith* Workbook

Susan M. Shaw

Smyth & Helwys Publishing, Inc.
6316 Peake Road
Macon, Georgia 31210-3960
1-800-747-3016

Library of Congress Cataloging-in-Publication Data

Shaw, Susan M. (Susan Maxine), 1960-
Reflective Faith Workbook : A Theological Toolbox for Women / by Susan M. Shaw.
pages cm
ISBN 978-1-57312-754-7 (pbk. : alk. paper)
1. Christian women--Religious life.
2. Bible--Criticism, interpretation, etc.
3. Theology--Study and teaching.
4. Women in Christianity. I. Title.
BV4527.S42197 2014
248.8'43--dc23

2014016330

Introduction

The exercises in this workbook will provide you with an opportunity to try out the tools discussed in the book. You may wish to start a journal to record your answers to workbook questions, create questions of your own, and write poems and stories as suggested in the exercises.

While the workbook has been created so you can complete all of the exercises on your own, the activities also lend themselves to group work. You may want to start a study group with friends or perhaps use the book and workbook for your curriculum for a church-based group. Some of the activities may be most effective in a group setting where you can share ideas and struggle together with questions. These activities are noted in the contents with a "G."

Some of the activities offer more challenge than others, and so the table of contents also notes the degree of challenge with one, two, or three fish.

One fish means the exercise is straightforward and can be completed fairly easily.

Two fish mean the exercise requires more thought or possible research in addition to the book and workbook.

Three fish mean the exercise asks you to think more deeply, challenge traditional ideas, use other resources, and push yourself to understand the content. Expect to spend more time completing these exercises.

The activities with this icon may require longer written responses or research. A separate journal may be useful for these activities, as well as for other personal reflection along the way.

While most exercises focus on the intellectual content of faith, they also encourage you to process your feelings about the topics, and they offer you occasions to think about how to apply what you're learning. Imagine these exercises as opportunities to learn new processes for thinking about the Bible and theology rather than as attempts to find the one right answer. These are tools for reflective Christians, activities to support your commitment to love God with your mind.

Contents

Map Your Faith Journey

The metaphor of a journey is common for one's experiences of faith across a lifetime. In the mid-1600s, John Bunyan wrote *Pilgrim's Progress*, an allegory in which the protagonist, Christian, leaves the City of Destruction to set out on a quest for the Celestial City. Along the way, he travels through places such as the Slough of Despond, the Valley of Humiliation, the Valley of the Shadow of Death, Vanity, Doubting Castle, and the Delectable Mountains. Eventually, accompanied by his friend Hopeful, Christian arrives in the land of Beulah and the Celestial City. Bunyan's negativity about most of the journey is reflective of a seventeenth-century orientation in that direction. Similarly, Hannah Hurnard's classic, *Hinds Feet on High Places*, sends our heroine Much-Afraid on a journey through the Desert, the Precipice Injury, the Shores of Loneliness, and the Valley of Loss before she reaches the Healing Streams and the High Places. Of course, our journeys have other possibilities as well. For many of us, while we may have faced our Sloughs of Despond, we have also rejoiced on the Mountain of Delight or relaxed in the Oasis of Peace. I imagine that for most of us, the journey has been a mix of moments of sadness or challenge or even despair as well as happiness, joy, and even ecstasy. This activity will help you reflect on your journey this far and imagine where you'd like to go from here.

Take a look at Thomas Conder's 1778 engraving of a map based on *Pilgrim's Progress*.

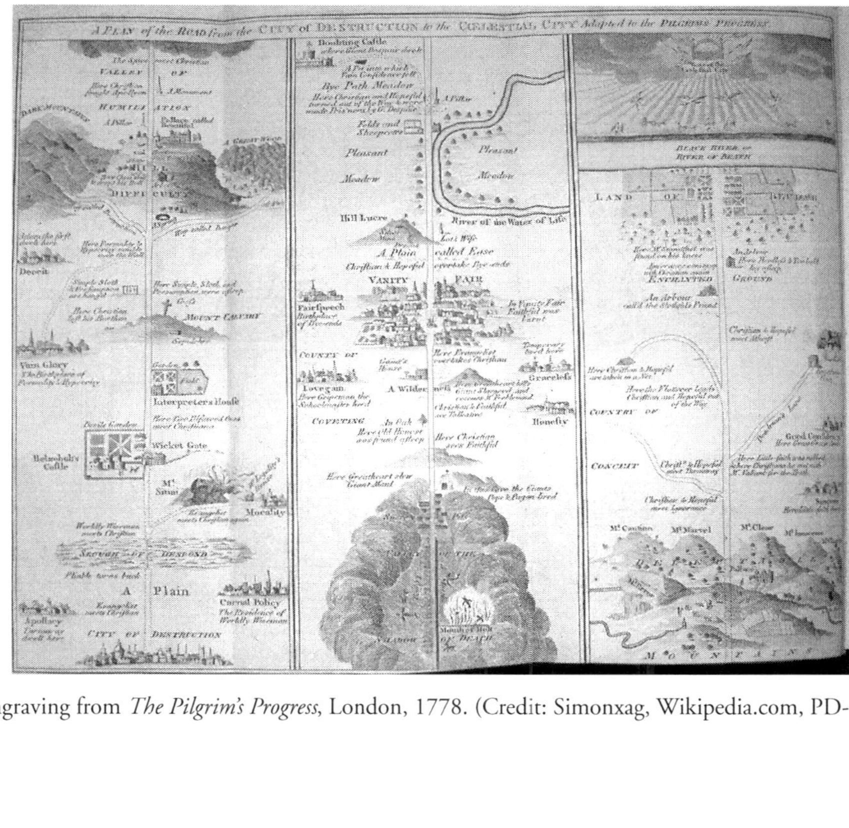

Engraving from *The Pilgrim's Progress*, London, 1778. (Credit: Simonxag, Wikipedia.com, PD-US)

Now think about your own journey of faith. Using paper and markers, draw a map of your faith journey from its beginning until now.

Questions

1. Where were your places of joy and peace?

2. At which places along your map have you had hard questions? How did you address those questions? Who helped you? Who didn't?

3. Are there places where you had to rethink something you believed because your experiences challenged it?

4. How have these questions changed you? Have you been able to use these questions as an opportunity to love God with your mind?

5. Are there places where gender was especially important? Were you ever excluded or limited by gender? Were you ever told that you were less than—less intelligent, less able, less worthy—because of gender? If so, how did those times make you feel? As you reflect on those times, what do they suggest to you about God, the church, humanity, and salvation? Do they raise other questions for you?

6. Are there places where larger social, cultural, or global issues intersected with your journey? How did your faith speak to these issues? Did these issues challenge any of your beliefs? What did you do about these issues? Have they left you with other questions?

Make a list of the questions you currently have about faith, the Bible, theology, church history, or ethics. When you finish reading *They Didn't Teach Me That in Sunday School,* come back to these questions and see if you have found new ways to think about the issues. Finally, imagine into your future. Where do you hope your journey takes you from here?

Exercise 2

Pinpoint Your Social Location

On the diagram below, write how you fit in each category. No one of these categories defines any person because all of them intersect and interact, shaping one another in our experiences. Your social location is at the center of these intersections—plus others, including where you live, the language(s) you speak, your education level, your employment, your marital status, and so on. Sometimes these categories confer unearned privilege on us. That is, we get things just by virtue of being in a particular category, for example. Other times, these categories confer unearned disadvantage on us; that is, we lose out on something just by virtue of being in a certain category.

Our social location gives us particular lenses by which we view the world. On the one hand, that means we have a unique and valuable perspective to bring to conversations about faith. On the other, it also means that our viewpoints are always partial, limited, and tentative, and so we need to approach the tasks of reading the Bible and doing theology with an openness to experiences and perspectives different from our own. It means we should always ask how our social locations affect how we think. It also means that we value both our own voices and the voices of others, while at the same time we recognize the inherent limitations of any person's perspective.

Think about your social location. How do you think your gender, race, social class, sexual identity, age, and abilities affect you? How do they shape who you are? How do you think your social location affects your experiences of God? Your views on theological issues?

Gender

____

Sexual Identity

____

Race

____

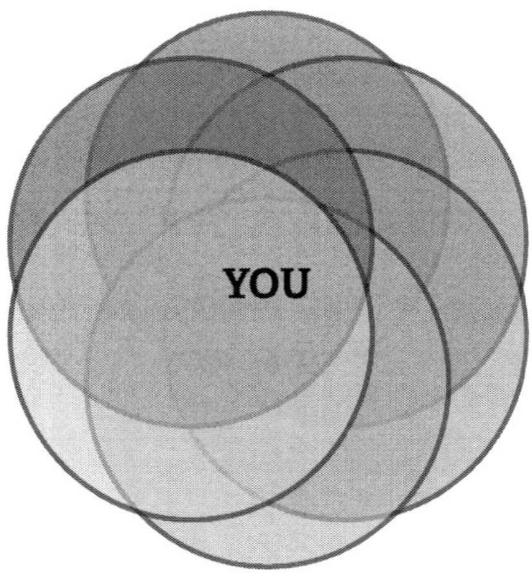

Ability

____

Social Class

____

Age

____

Exercise 3

Write a Letter to God

Many people write letters to God as a way to ask for something, wrestle with a problem, or offer thanks. Think about where you are in your faith journey. What are your struggles? What limits you? Where do you need to grow? Where do you have questions? What are your joys? For what are you thankful?

Write a letter to God, laying out your struggles and questions. Write about difficulties you face, fears you have, and pain and suffering you experience. Express your joy and gratitude for the positive elements of your life.

After you finish your letter, read it out loud. Then sit with the silence for a while and listen.

In Sue Monk Kidd's novel, *The Secret Life of Bees*, one of the characters who is often overwhelmed by the world's misery has a "wailing wall" in her backyard. When she is overcome with emotion, she writes it all down and then tucks the piece of paper in her wailing wall. Find yourself a "wailing wall." I once used a stack of firewood for mine. Maybe yours could be the books along your bookshelf or the rocks in a stone wall. Put your letter in the wailing wall and offer it up to God as a prayer. Then leave it there.

Throughout your day, practice attentiveness to the presence of God in the silence and the noise around you. Attune your ears to the still, small voice by listening carefully for it.

Exercise 4

The Four Resurrection Accounts

Often our expectations about what the Bible says reflect what we've been told rather than a close reading of the text itself. For example, our sense of the resurrection story likely comes from some combination of the four accounts we find in the Gospel but does not take note of the differences in the stories. This exercise will allow you to make a side-by-side comparison of the accounts, noticing the similarities and differences. It will also help you think about the women in the stories. Unless noted otherwise, all scripture passages are from the NRSV.

Compare and contrast these four accounts. What surprises you?

Matthew 28

(1) After the sabbath, as the first day of the week was dawning, Mary Magdalene and the other Mary went to see the tomb. (2) And suddenly there was a great earthquake; for an angel of the Lord, descending from heaven, came and rolled back the stone and sat on it. (3) His appearance was like lightning, and his clothing white as snow. (4) For fear of him the guards shook and became like dead men. (5) But the angel said to the women, "Do not be afraid; I know that you are looking for Jesus who was crucified. (6) He is not here; for he has been raised, as he said. Come, see the place where he lay. (7) Then go quickly and tell his disciples, 'He has been raised from the dead, and indeed he is going ahead of you to Galilee; there you will see him.' This is my message for you." (8) So they left the tomb quickly with fear and great joy, and ran to tell his disciples. (9) Suddenly Jesus met them and said, "Greetings!" And they came to him, took hold of his feet, and worshiped him. (10) Then Jesus said to them, "Do not be afraid; go and tell my brothers to go to Galilee; there they will see me."

Mark 16

(1) When the sabbath was over, Mary Magdalene, and Mary the mother of James, and Salome bought spices, so that they might go and anoint him. (2) And very early on the first day of the week, when the sun had risen, they went to the tomb. (3) They had been saying to one another, "Who will roll away the stone for us from the entrance to the tomb?" (4) When they looked up, they saw that the stone, which was very large, had already been rolled back. (5) As they entered the tomb, they saw a young man, dressed in a white robe, sitting on the right side; and they were alarmed. (6) But he said to them, "Do not be alarmed; you are looking for Jesus of Nazareth, who was crucified. He has been raised; he is not here. Look, there is the place they laid him. (7) But go, tell his disciples and Peter that he is going ahead of you to Galilee; there you will see him, just as he told you." (8) So they went out and fled from the tomb, for terror and amazement had seized them; and they said nothing to anyone, for they were afraid.

Luke 24

(1) But on the first day of the week, at early dawn, they came to the tomb, taking the spices that they had prepared. (2) They found the stone rolled away from the tomb, (3) but when they went in, they

did not find the body. (4) While they were perplexed about this, suddenly two men in dazzling clothes stood beside them. (5) The women were terrified and bowed their faces to the ground, but the men said to them, "Why do you look for the living among the dead? He is not here, but has risen. (6) Remember how he told you, while he was still in Galilee, (7) that the Son of Man must be handed over to sinners, and be crucified, and on the third day rise again." (8) Then they remembered his words, (9) and returning from the tomb, they told all this to the eleven and to all the rest. (10) Now it was Mary Magdalene, Joanna, Mary the mother of James, and the other women with them who told this to the apostles. (11) But these words seemed to them an idle tale, and they did not believe them. (12) But Peter got up and ran to the tomb; stooping and looking in, he saw the linen cloths by themselves; then he went home, amazed at what had happened.

John 20

(1) Early on the first day of the week, while it was still dark, Mary Magdalene came to the tomb and saw that the stone had been removed from the tomb. (2) So she ran and went to Simon Peter and the other disciple, the one whom Jesus loved, and said to them, "They have taken the Lord out of the tomb, and we do not know where they have laid him." (3) Then Peter and the other disciple set out and went towards the tomb. (4) The two were running together, but the other disciple outran Peter and reached the tomb first. (5) He bent down to look in and saw the linen wrappings lying there, but he did not go in. (6) Then Simon Peter came, following him, and went into the tomb. He saw the linen wrappings lying there, (7) and the cloth that had been on Jesus' head, not lying with the linen wrappings but rolled up in a place by itself. (8) Then the other disciple, who reached the tomb first, also went in, and he saw and believed; (9) for as yet they did not understand the scripture, that he must rise from the dead. (10) Then the disciples returned to their homes.

Questions

1. Why are the accounts different?

2. What problems might arise if someone tried to create a single account, arguing that all four accounts describe the events with historical accuracy?

3. What do these stories suggest about women's discipleship? What do you learn from these women?

Notice the women in the accounts. How are they portrayed? Write your own version of the women's story.

Exercise 5

The Authoritative Text: An Exercise in Textual Criticism

Before beginning to translate the biblical text, scholars have to establish an authoritative text, the text they believe most closely resembles the original manuscripts of the biblical books. Remember that we do not have the original manuscripts. At best, we have copies of copies of copies of copies. Sometimes we have fragments of copies. A number of varying manuscripts exist, and scholars must deal with issues that arise from the ways books were copied by hand before the advent of the printing press, such as errors caused by mishearing a word as the text was read, accidental repeating or omission of words, or even intentional changes that made a passage more acceptable to a copyist. Additionally, in the case of ancient Greek, writers used all capital letters, no spaces, and no punctuation. The following exercise will help you imagine what determining the authoritative text must be like. You will try to decide the authoritative text of part of a speech given by suffragist and abolitionist Julia Ward Howe.

Below are three variant texts of Julia Ward Howe's 1893 speech, "What Is Religion?" Examine the passages closely and try to figure out which is the authoritative text. Compare them for agreements. Note possible errors such as repetition or omission of words, misspellings, and grammatical errors. Look for intentional changes that might reflect the thoughts of a later editor. Then, on a separate piece of paper, write what you think is the authoritative text of this passage. You can find the original text at the end of this workbook.

Questions

1. What did you learn about the process of determining the authoritative biblical text from this exercise?

2. Why do you think it's important to understand that there is a process for deciding which biblical text is likely closest to the original text?

Variant 1: The New York Manuscript

ITHINKNOTHINGISRELIGIONWHICHPUTSONEINDIVIDUALABSO-
LUTELYABOVEOTHERSANDSURELYNOTHINGISRELIGIONWHICHPUTSONESECTABO
VEANOTHERRELIGIONISISPRIMARILYOURRELATIONTOTHESUPREMETOGODHIM-
SELFITISFORHIMTOJUDGEITISFORHIMTOSAYWHEREWEBELONGWHOISHIGHESTAN
DWHOISNOTOFTHATWEKNOWNOTHINGANANYRELIGIONWHICHWILLSACRI-
FICEACERTAINSETOFHUMANBEINGSFORTHEENJOYMENTORAGGRANDIZEMENTOR
ADVANTAGEOFANOTHERISNORELIGIONITISATHINGWHICHMAYBEALLOWEDBUTI-
TISAGAINSTTRUERELIGIONANYRELIGIONWHICHSACRIFICESWOMENTOTHEBRUTA
LITYOFMENISNORELIGION

Variant 2: The Rhode Island Manuscript

ITHINKNOTHINGISRELIGIONWHICHPUTSONEINDIVIDUALABSO-
LUTELYABOVEOTHERSANDSURELYNOTHINGIFRELIGIONWHICHPUTSONESEXABOV
EANOTHERRELIGIONISPRIMARILYOURRELATIONTOTHESUPREMETOGODHWE-
SELFITISFORHERTOJUDGEITISFORHERTOSAYWHEREWEBELONGWHOISHIGHESTAN
DWHOISNOTOFTHATWEKNOWNOTHINGANDANYRELIGIONWHICHWILLSACRI-
FICEACERTAINSETOFHUMANBEINGSFORTHEEENJOYMENTORAGGRANDIZEMENTO
RADVANTAGEOFANOTHERISNOTRELIGIONITISATHINGWHICHMAYBEALLOWEDBU-
TITISAGAINSTTRUERELIGIONANYRELIGIONWHICHSACRIFICESWOMENTOTHEBRU
TALITYOFMENISNORRELIGION

Variant 3: The Boston Manuscript

ITHINKNOTTHINGISRELIGIONWHICHPUTSONEINDIVIDUALABSO-
LUTELYABOVEOTHERSANDSURELYNOTHINGISRELIGIONWHICHPUTSONESEXABOV
ETHEOTHERRELIGIONISPRIMARYOURRELATIONTOTHESUPREMETOGODHIMSELFI-
TISFORHIMTOJUDGEITISFORHIMTOSAYWHEREWEBELONGWHOISHIGHESTANDW
HOISISNOTOFTHATWENONOTHINGANDANYRELIGIONWHICHSACRIFICESACER-
TAINSETOFHUMANBEINGSFORTHEENJOYMENTORAGGRANDIZEMENTORADVANTA
GEOFANOTHERISNORELIGIONITISATHINGWHICHMAYBEALLOWEDBUTITISAGAIN-
STTRUERELIGIONANYRELIGIONWHICHSACRIFICESWOMENTOTHEBRUTALITYOFM
ENISNOTRELIGION

Exercise 6

Comparing Translations

The original languages of the Bible are Hebrew, Greek, and Aramaic. Our English versions are translations, renderings from the original languages that try to convey the original meaning of the text as closely as possible. Because translation is never a simple word-for-word process, translators make judgment calls about how best to capture the meaning of the original language. This exercise helps you examine the impact of these judgment calls on how we understand a text once it's rendered in English.

1. Below are three translations of Romans 8:28. How are they different? How might each translation change our understanding of the passage?

> **King James Version**
> And we know that all things work together for good to them that love God, to them who are the called according to his purpose.
>
> **New International Version**
> And we know that in all things God works for the good of those who love him, who have been called according to his purpose.
>
> **New American Standard Bible**
> And we know that God causes all things to work together for good to those who love God, to those who are called according to His purpose.

Select a biblical passage that is important to you. Then read it in each of these three translations. You can find these versions online at http://www.biblegateway.com. What do you learn by comparing and contrasting these passages? Take a look at your passage in the Wyclif or Douay-Rheims translations. Then look at it in the Good News Bible. What do you notice? How do you think changes in the English language itself affect translations and our reading of translations?

2. Compare and contrast Amos 1:1 from the NRSV and the Living Bible, which is a paraphrase.

New Revised Standard Version
The words of Amos, who was among the shepherds of Tekoa, which he saw concerning Israel in the days of King Uzziah of Judah and in the days of King Jeroboam son of Joash of Israel, two years before the earthquake.

The Living Bible
Amos was a herdsman living in the village of Tekoa. All day long he sat on the hillsides watching the sheep, keeping them from straying. One day, in a vision, God told him some of the things that were going to happen to his nation, Israel. This vision came to him at the time Uzziah was king of Judah, and while Jeroboam (son of Joash) was king of Israel—two years before the earthquake.

Why do you think a paraphrase might be problematic?

3. Why might this kind of comparison work be important for you in your own study of the Bible?

Exercise 7

Identifying Sources I: An Exercise in the Documentary Hypothesis

This exercise will give you the opportunity to identify the various sources used by the redactors (editors) of the Pentateuch (the first five books of the Bible). Remember that these redactors were working with a wide variety of materials that had been handed down through different traditions. The original authors had written for specific reasons to particular audiences, and, when the redactors put their books together, they were writing for a specific audience in specific circumstances, and so they used the materials to make points for their audiences in their contexts. The following specific examples should help you see how the redactors used the sources and interwove them to make their points. This exercise will help you understand how biblical scholars came to recognize that there were a number of redactors and the redactors were working with a variety of sources.

1. Read the following passages and make a list of the characteristics of each passage—its literary style, its use of descriptive language, its major concerns, its descriptions of and names for God, etc.

- Genesis 11:1-9

- Exodus 20:1-26

- Genesis 11:10-27

- Genesis 41:1-45

- Exodus 6:2-9

• Deuteronomy 5:1-22

2. Next, compare and contrast the following pairs of passages (and one trio). Make a list of your observations for each pair.

• Exodus 20:1-17 and Deuteronomy 5:1-21

• Genesis 16:1-15 and Genesis 21:1-21

• Exodus 16 and Numbers 11

• Genesis 21:25-31 and Genesis 26:26-33

• Genesis 12:10-20; Genesis 20; and Genesis 26:6-11

Taking activities 1 and 2 into consideration, what does the exercise suggest to you about the authorship of the Pentateuch?

Exercise 8

Identifying Sources II

Having noticed the stylistic and literary differences you found in Exercise 7, scholars recognized that whoever wrote the final version of the Pentateuch was working from a variety of sources, much like a student writing a term paper. As they studied the text, scholars identified four primary sources. This identification is known as the "Documentary Hypothesis" (While scholars hypothesize that the sources may be more complicated (such as a JE source that already combined two of the sources before the redactors used them to create the text as we have it, the "four source hypothesi"s forms the generally accepted basis for examining the sources of the Pentateuch). The four sources and their characteristics are below:

I. J or Yahwist

a. The primary characteristic of the J source is the use of "Yahweh," the personal name for God. In English, Yahweh is translated "LORD God."

b. J is marked by colorful folk narrative style.

c. God is described in human-like terms.

d. Stories do not offer interpretive comment.

e. The J source has a pattern of promise and fulfillment.

f. The perspective of the J source is always a human one.

g. Stories have dramatic suspense and center on crises.

II. E or Elohist

a. The Elohist uses the name "Elohim" for God. In English the term is translated as "God."

b. The E source is usually closely interwoven with the J source.

c. E avoids describing God in human-like terms. Instead, angels and dreams are used as the means of divine revelation.

III. D or Deuteronomist

a. The Deuteronomist is concerned with Israel's faithfulness to the law.

b. D material often sounds like a sermon and uses phrases such as "Hear, O Israel," "Remember," "Take heed," and "Keep all the commandments."

c. D follows a theological formula—obedience brings reward and disobedience brings punishment.

d. D explains Israel's election as a matter of God's love.

e. D believes that the center of Israel's worship should be in one place.

f. D is easy to find. It's only the book of Deuteronomy.

IV. P or Priestly

a. P is marked by concern for the interests of the priesthood and religious structures.

b. P is concerned with rituals, laws, genealogies, and chronological details of Israel's past.
c. P's style is marked by phrases such as "These are the generations," "after its kinds," and "be fruitful and multiply."
d. In P, God is wholly other and glorified in the created order.
e. P avoids using human-like language to talk about God. Encounters with God are explained simply, without elaboration, and with phrases such as "God called" or "God said."

Below are the passages you examined in Exercise 7 along with the sources of each passage. See if you can identify why each passage has been assigned its particular source. In other words, what is it about the passage that matches the descriptions of the characteristics of J, E, D, and P described above.

- Genesis 11:1-9 (J)

- Exodus 20:1-26 (E)

- Genesis 11:10-27 (P)

- Genesis 41:1-45 (E)

- Exodus 6:2-9 (P)

- Deuteronomy 5:1-22 (D)

- Exodus 20:1-17 (E) and Deuteronomy 5:1-21 (D)

- Genesis 16:1-15 (J) and Genesis 21:1-21 (E)

- Exodus 16 (P) and Numbers 11 (J)

- Genesis 21:25-31 (E) and Genesis 26:26-33 (J)

- Genesis 12:10-20 (J); Genesis 20 (E); and Genesis 26:6-11 (J)

What do you learn from identifying the sources of various passages? Why might this process be important for your understanding of Scripture?

Exercise 9

Identifying Sources III

Now it's your turn. Based on the characteristics outlined in Exercise 8, try to identify the source for each of the following passages from the NRSV:

_____ 1. And he dreamed that there was a ladder set up on the earth, the top of it reaching to heaven; and the angels of God were ascending and descending on it.

_____ 2. Then God said, "Let there be light"; and there was light.

_____ 3. They heard the sound of the LORD God walking in the garden at the time of the evening breeze, and the man and his wife hid themselves from the presence of the Lord God among the trees of the garden.

_____ 4. When Jared had lived one hundred sixty-two years he became the father of Enoch.

_____ 5. you shall seek the place that the LORD your God will choose out of all your tribes as his habitation to put his name there.

_____ 6. This is the ritual of the burnt-offering. The burnt-offering itself shall remain on the hearth upon the altar all night until the morning, while the fire on the altar shall be kept burning.

_____ 7. While my glory passes by I will put you in a cleft of the rock, and I will cover you with my hand until I have passed by; then I will take away my hand, and you shall see my back; but my face shall not be seen.

_____ 8. After these things the word of the LORD came to Abram in a vision, "Do not be afraid, Abram, I am your shield; your reward shall be very great."

_____ 9. Now these are the names of the Israelites, Jacob and his offspring, who came to Egypt.

_____ 10. Hear, O Israel: The LORD is our God, the LORD alone. You shall love the LORD your God with all your heart, and with all your soul, and with all your might.

Source criticism is important because it helps us understand the origins and intentions of those who first recorded stories, laws, and rituals. In the next exercise, we'll look at source criticism in the New Testament.

Exercise 10

The Sermon on the Mount: An Exercise in Source Criticism

Most biblical scholars suggest that the writers of the Synoptic Gospels (Matthew, Mark, and Luke) were working with some shared primary sources. Most scholars agree that Mark is the oldest Gospel (written around 70 CE) and was one of the sources used by Matthew and Luke. Luke (written around 70–90 CE) and Matthew (written around 85–90 CE) each have unique source material (known as L and M) that does not show up in any of the other Gospels. Finally, scholars hypothesize a fourth source, usually called "Q" (from the German word *Quelle*, meaning "source"), that is the source of material common to Matthew and Luke but not found in Mark. We do not have a copy of Q, but scholars have attempted to reconstruct it from the common Matthew and Luke materials, although there is no agreement on what exactly should be contained in Q.

What we commonly call "the Sermon on the Mount" in Matthew 5:1–7:29 appears as "the Sermon on the Plain" in Luke 6:17-49. In Matthew's account, the sermon occurs before Jesus calls the twelve disciples, but it is after their call in Luke. Matthew includes a lot of material in his version of the sermon, while Luke includes some of it here and some of it in other places throughout his book. While the sermon is not part of Mark's Gospel, some of its content can be found there.

1. Compare the following passages. What material is common to all three Gospels? This is to identify the Markan material (material Matthew and Luke borrowed from Mark's Gospel):

Matt 5:13	Luke 6:20b-23	Mark 9:49-50
Matt 5:14-16	Luke 8:16	Mark 4:21
Matt 5:27-32	Luke 16:18	Mark 9:43-48
Matt 6:7-15	Luke 11:1-4	Mark 11:25-26
Matt 7:1-5	Luke 6:37-42	Mark 4:24-25

2. Next, go through Matthew 5:1–7:29 and Luke 6:17-49 and identify the material they have in common with each other but not with Mark. This material is likely from Q. Note also the common material that is throughout Luke but not in the Sermon on the Plain: Luke 11:9-13; 11:34-36; 12:22-32; 12:33-34; 12:57-59; 13:23-24; 16:13; 16:16-17; 16:18.

3. Finally, go back through the two passages and identify the material that is in Matthew but not in Luke, and then do the same for the material that is in Luke but not in Matthew. The first set, then, is from M, the material unique to Matthew, and the second set is from L, the material unique to Luke.

Questions

1. How does source criticism challenge the notion of the Gospels as primarily factual and historical accounts of the life of Jesus?

2. If historical accuracy was not the primary goal of the writers, why do you think they used the material the way they did?

3. Why do you think it might be important for you to understand the sources of the New Testament?

Exercise 11

Name that Pericope

While source criticism examines the written sources used by the Bible's writers and editors, we recognize that much of the content of the Bible circulated in oral form long before it was written down. Form criticism analyzes the oral tradition of Scripture, paying special attention to the various genres of the biblical material as it would have been transmitted orally.

Pericope (pə'-ri-kə-pe): A small literary unit or genre, such as a saying or miracle story, that existed independently in oral tradition and has been tied together with other pericopae by an editor to form the Gospels as we know them.

Framework Material: The connecting sentences that tie pericopae together and give the whole book a narrative structure but are not part of the original pericopae

Genres of the Synoptic Gospels (Matthew, Mark, Luke)
Scholars have identified a number of literary forms in the Gospels. This section provides a brief outline of some of those forms.

I. Sayings—phrases that express an idea people generally hold to be true. Several types of sayings are identified below.

A. Proverbs/Wisdom Sayings—timeless religious truths and practical wisdom to apply in daily living

B. Prophetic and Apocalyptic Sayings—refer to the present, the in-breaking of God's realm, not a future event; call to repentance with promise of salvation to those who are prepared and woe to those who are unrepentant

C. Legal Sayings/Church Rules—parallel the preaching of the prophets against external piety and legalism, promote obedience to the will of God

D. "I" Sayings—references to the person of Jesus

E. Similitudes (points of comparison) and Similar Forms

1. Hyperbole (exaggeration)
2. Paradox (two seemingly opposite things that are both true)
3. Comparisons/images/figures/similes
4. Metaphor (figure of speech in which one object represents another)

II. Parables—stories that are characterized by an internal juxtaposition—positioning two ideas up against one another in an unexpected way so as to create a sense of surprise or shock for the listener

New Testament form critics seek to identify the life setting of Jesus (*sitz im leben jesu*) as a way to help us understand the parables. The life setting offers an explanation for why Jesus told that particular parable. Often these life settings are criticism for Jesus' lifestyle, ministry, and preaching, scholarly debates, or teaching opportunities.

III. Miracle Stories—stories that demonstrate Jesus' messianic authority through the unconscious display of his nature. In other words, the miracles are not supernatural events called down by Jesus but rather involuntary manifestations of his character.

A. Exorcisms
B. Healings
C. Nature wonders
D. Resuscitations

IV. Controversy Stories—stories that provide a framework for an important saying of Jesus, usually in response to a question

A. Types of controversies/dialogues
  1. Occasioned by Jesus' healing
  2. Occasioned by the conduct of Jesus and/or the disciples
  3. Questions by the disciples or others
  4. Questions by opponents

V. Passion Narratives—the stories of Jesus' suffering following the Last Supper and through the crucifixion

Your Turn: Identify the framework material and the pericopae in the following passage from Luke 20 by drawing a box around each pericope and highlighting the framework material.

1 One day, as he was teaching the people in the temple and telling the good news, the chief
priests and the scribes came with the elders 2 and said to him, "Tell us, by what authority are
you doing these things? Who is it that gave you this authority?" 3 He answered them, "I will
also ask you a question, and you tell me: 4 Did the baptism of John come from heaven, or was
it of human origin?" 5 They discussed it with one another, saying, "If we say, 'From heaven,' he
will say, 'Why did you not believe him?' 6 But if we say, 'Of human origin,' all the people will
stone us; for they are convinced that John was a prophet." 7 So they answered that they did not
know where it came from. 8 Then Jesus said to them, "Neither will I tell you by what authority
I am doing these things." 9 He began to tell the people this parable: "A man planted a vineyard,

and leased it to tenants, and went to another country for a long time. [10]When the season came, he sent a slave to the tenants in order that they might give him his share of the produce of the vineyard; but the tenants beat him and sent him away empty-handed. [11]Next he sent another slave; that one also they beat and sent away empty-handed. [12]And he sent still a third; this one also they wounded and threw out. [13]Then the owner of the vineyard said, 'What shall I do? I will send my beloved son; perhaps they will respect him.' [14]But when the tenants saw him, they discussed it among themselves and said, 'This is the heir; let us kill him so that the inheritance may be ours.' [15]So they threw him out of the vineyard and killed him. What then will the owner of the vineyard do to them? [16]He will come and destroy those tenants and give the vineyard to others." When they heard this, they said, "Heaven forbid!" [17]But he looked at them and said, "What then does this text mean: 'The stone that the builders rejected has become the cornerstone'? [18]Everyone who falls on that stone will be broken to pieces; and it will crush anyone on whom it falls." [19]When the scribes and chief priests realized that he had told this parable against them, they wanted to lay hands on him at that very hour, but they feared the people.

Questions

1. Why do you think the redactor/editor put these pericopae together in this particular way?

2. How does understanding the construction of the passage as an edited work of pericopae and framework material help you interpret the intent of the redactor? In other words, how does it help you understand better what the redactor intended for his audience to get out of the story as he told it?

Two Ways of Being: The Conventional and Unconventional in Jesus' Parables

1. The parables of Jesus challenge us to see two possibilities for being in the world, one the conventional way of the world and the other the unconventional way of God's realm. Use the chart below to identify in each parable the conventional way and the way of God's realm.

Parable	Conventional Way of Being	Unconventional Way of Being
The Treasure Hidden in a Field (Matt 13:44)		
The Pearl of Great Value (Matt 13:45-46)		
The Unforgiving Servant (Matt 18:23-35)		
The Two Sons (Matt 21:28-31)		
The Ten Bridesmaids (Matt 25:1-13)		
The Mustard Seed (Mark 4:30-32)		
The Good Samaritan (Luke 10:30-35)		
The Rich Fool (Luke 12:16-21)		
The Great Dinner (Luke 14:16-24)		
The Pharisee and the Tax Collector (Luke 18:10-14)		

2. Flannery O'Connor, a devout Christian and fiction writer from Georgia, wrote, "All human nature vigorously resists grace because grace changes us and the change is painful" (*The Habit of Being: The Letters of Flannery O'Connor* [New York: Macmillan, 1988] 307).

How might her observation describe the contrast between conventional and unconventional ways of being in the parables?

3. In *The Cost of Discipleship* ([New York: Simon & Schuster, 2012] 44), Dietrich Bonhoeffer wrote,

> Cheap grace is the grace we bestow on ourselves. Cheap grace is the preaching of forgiveness without requiring repentance, baptism without church discipline, Communion without confession. . . . Cheap grace is grace without discipleship, grace without the cross, grace without Jesus Christ, living and incarnate. . . . Costly grace is the gospel which must be sought again and again and again, the gift which must be asked for, the door at which a man must knock. Such grace is costly because it calls us to follow, and it is grace because it calls us to follow Jesus Christ. It is costly because it costs a man his life, and it is grace because it gives a man the only true life. It is costly because it condemns sin, and grace because it justifies the sinner.

How do the images of conventional and unconventional ways of being mirror Bonhoeffer's notions of cheap and costly grace?

4. Read the following quotations from Annie Dillard.

> On the whole, I do not find Christians, outside of the catacombs, sufficiently sensible of conditions. Does anyone have the foggiest idea what sort of power we so blithely invoke? Or, as I suspect, does no one believe a word of it? The churches are children playing on the floor with their chemistry sets, mixing up a batch of TNT to kill a Sunday morning. It is madness to wear ladies' straw hats and velvet hats to church; we should all be wearing crash helmets. Ushers should issue life preservers and signal flares; they should lash us to our pews. For the sleeping god may wake someday and take offense, or the waking god may draw us out to where we can never return. . . . (*Teaching a Stone to Talk: Expeditions and Encounters* [New York: Harper & Row, 1982] 40–41)

> There is always an enormous temptation in all of life to diddle around making itsy-bitsy friends and meals and journeys for itsy-bitsy years on end. . . . We are making hay when we should be making

> whoopee; we are raising tomatoes when we should be raising Cain, or Lazarus. (*Pilgrim at Tinker Creek* [New York: Bantam, 1974] 276)

What do you think she is suggesting about what it means for us to choose the unconventional way of being?

How does she critique the complacency of the conventional way?

5. What do these images of conventional and unconventional ways of being in the world mean to you? Are there places in your life where you can identify choices between conventional and unconventional ways of being? What do these parables say to you?

Write a story about a time you faced an important decision and chose the unconventional way of being in the world. Reflect on that story and the impact your choice has had on you.

Exercise 13

The Parable of the Widow and the Unjust Judge: An Exercise in Form and Redaction Criticism

While form criticism traces the oral development of small units of biblical material (pericopae), redaction criticism examines the role of the redactor, the editor, who put the biblical book in its final form. Redaction criticism helps us understand why the redactor put the book together the way he did and what he was trying to say to his target audience through the editorial choices he made.

Read the parable of the widow and the unjust judge found in Luke 18:1-8.

The Literary Dimension of the Parable

1. What is the parable's surprising comparison (internal juxtaposition)?

2. What shock does the parable create by putting conventional and unconventional ways of being alongside one another?

The Historical Setting of the Parable

1. What is the life setting of Jesus *(sitz im leben jesu)* for the parable?

2. Why might the redactor/editor have placed the parable at this point in the narrative? Look at chapter 17 and the rest of chapter 18. How does Luke frame and interpret the story within the larger narrative of the book?

3. How does reading the parable as a stand-alone story and reading it within Luke's interpretive framework offer multiple possible and valid readings of the story?

4. What was the life setting (*sitz im leben*) of the Christian movement to whom the book was written?

5. How might the life setting (*sitz im leben*) of the contemporary reader affect the reading of the parable?

The Educational Purpose of the Parable

1. What does the parable teach us about God's coming and present realm (What is the eschatological dimension of the parable)?

2. What does the parable tell us about authentic and inauthentic existence (What is the existential dimension of the parable)?

3. How does the parable suggest people treat one another (What is the ethical dimension of the parable)?

4. What decision does the parable demand of its hearers (What is the evangelistic dimension of the parable)?

The Parable and the Reader

1. In this parable, the widow acts against the expected norms for women in her day. Do you identify with the widow in the story?

2. What might her story say to contemporary women?

3. What does it say to you? What decision does it demand of you?

Write the story of the widow from her perspective. How might she have told her own story?

The Story of Ruth: An Exercise in Narrative Criticism

The book of Ruth is a well-crafted short story set during the period of the Judges, and it provides us with an excellent opportunity to practice narrative criticism. Read the book one time to re-familiarize yourself with its basic story. Then, using the prompts below, go back through the book to explore it in more depth. Having a good commentary on hand may prove useful in helping you understand the customs and the interesting sexual tensions that are an integral part of the story.

1. Although the book of Ruth seems simple on its surface, the story is actually complex and rich. The plot itself operates on a number of levels. Reread the story and identify how the plot operates as:

    a. a romance story

    b. a story about law and legal commitments

    c. a story about morality

    d. a story about family

    e. a story about nation

2. Describe the narrator of the book. What does the narrator know or not know? From what perspective or point of view does the narrator tell the story? What does the narrator want readers to get out of the story?

3. What are the settings of the book? What do we know about each of these settings? Do these settings play a role elsewhere in the Bible? If so, what might these settings mean for this particular story?

4. What is the atmosphere of the story? How does the atmosphere reflect the story? How does it help move the story along?

5. The characters are developed through their words and actions. Look at each of the major characters in the story—Naomi, Ruth, and Boaz—and answer the following questions:

a. What do we know about the character's background? What does that suggest to us about the nature of the character?

b. What does the character say? What do the character's words indicate about the character?

c. What does the character do? What do the character's actions indicate about the character?

d. In what ways does the character challenge the conventional thinking of the day? In what ways does the character reflect the conventional thinking of the day?

e. How do the characters relate to one another?

f. What role does the story give God as a character? How else does God show up in the story?

6. Most commentators agree that the theme of Ruth is loyalty and loving-kindness (*chesed* in Hebrew). *Chesed* describes God's relationship to Israel or the relationship among family members or a community. How do you see this theme developed in the book of Ruth? How do each of the major characters demonstrate *chesed*?

7. Some commentators read the book of Ruth from perspectives other than the dominant American one. For example, an Asian feminist biblical critic warns the story has a dark side for Asian women who have already been socialized to serve mothers and mothers-in-law and obey elders rather than to choose the lives they desire (Anna May Say Pa, "Reading Ruth 3:1-5 from an Asian Woman's Perspective," *Engaging the Bible in a Gendered World*, eds. Linda Day and Carolyn Pressler [Louisville: Westminster John Knox, 2006] 47–59). How does your social context influence the way you read the story? What are the various possible readings of the story from your own social location and life experiences?

8. What does the book of Ruth mean to you as a contemporary reader? What can you learn from Ruth that applies to your own life?

Exercise 15

Should Women Keep Silent?: An Exercise in Historical-Critical Reading

First Corinthians 14:33-36 is often cited as proof that women should not be allowed to speak in church. The outline that follows uses the tools of historical criticism and will help you study the passage in greater detail.

> 33for God is a God not of disorder but of peace. (As in all the churches of the saints, 34women should be
> silent in the churches. For they are not permitted to speak, but should be subordinate, as the law also
> says. 35If there is anything they desire to know, let them ask their husbands at home. For it is shameful
> for a woman to speak in church. 36Or did the word of God originate with you? Or are you the only ones
> it has reached?)

I. How have you heard this passage used?

II. Did Paul actually write these verses?

1. Textual. In some manuscripts, these verses are at the end of the chapter, raising the question of whether or not a later reader added them as a marginal note that a later scribe then copied into the manuscript. Another possibility is that a copier left them out and a later scribe corrected the manuscript by adding them back in but in the wrong place.

2. Paul's Theology. Compare these passages with Paul's writing in 1 Corinthians 11:2-6; Philippians 4:2-3; Romans 16:3; 16:6; 16:7; 16:1. What similarities/differences do you find?

3. The Pastoral Letters. Compare the theology of these verses with 1 Timothy and Titus. These pastoral letters, although attributed to Paul, were likely written by later followers of Paul. Some scholars suggest that 1 Corinthians 14:33-36 is more in keeping with the theology of the writer of the pastoral letters than with Paul. What do you think?

III. Here are a number of ways various scholars have explained this passage. Do any of these interpretations seem persuasive to you?

1. Quoting Troublemakers. Throughout 1 Corinthians, Paul quotes the Corinthians and corrects them (6:12; 7:1-2; 8:1; 8:4-6). Might Paul be doing the same in the passage? In the other passages, however, the quotations and Paul's response are much more clearly marked.

2. Addressing a Specific Problem in a Specific Church. Look at Paul's comments on hair in chapter 11. Most contemporary readers, even conservative readers, do not understand these comments as applying to all people in all times. Might Paul's comments on women be understood as addressing a particular problem in the church at Corinth—specifically women converts bringing ecstatic cultic practices into the church, which Paul would have seen as disruptive? Most scholars find a great deal of Paul's argument in chapter 11 to be convoluted, but, interestingly, Paul seems to want to make sure that his directives about the proper order of prophesying do not imply women's inferiority. In 11:11 ("In the Lord woman is not independent of man or man independent of woman"), most translations stress the interdependence of woman and man in the Lord, but one scholar argues that this translation is questionable. He suggests that the term translated as "independent" is better rendered "different from" or "unlike." This means the verse would read, "In the Lord woman is not different from man nor man from woman" (this translation of 11:11 is also more consistent with Paul's theology expressed in Galatians 3:28, where he asserts that in Christ there is no longer male nor female). So Paul is not arguing for a difference between women and men but for different customs for women and men that mark them as distinct from cultic worshipers of the day. Again, this reading of 11:11 strengthens the argument that Paul is not suggesting that his demand for silence among women in 14:34-35 be for all women in all times but rather is directing his comments to a specific problem in the Corinthian church.

3. Making Distinctions among Women. Look at how Paul addresses unmarried women in chapter 7. In chapter 14, might he be addressing only married women who had challenged their husbands in public (a practice frowned upon by Romans)? Would this, however, be inconsistent with Paul's attitude toward married women like Prisca and Junia?

4. Defending His Own Authority. Why, in his culture and time, would Paul have felt the need to silence women? Perhaps, empowered by their experience of the gospel, these women were exercising great influence on the church at Corinth. Verse 36 suggests that these women see themselves as having the ability to speak for God, and by so doing they challenge Paul's exclusive claim to do so. Perhaps Paul is exerting his authority over them and trying to shame them into silence.

5. Arguing for Propriety. Throughout the book of 1 Corinthians, Paul is concerned with order in the church and with setting the church apart from the cultic worship prevalent throughout the empire. How might these verses in chapter 14 be read to address the issue of propriety in worship and distance from the ecstatic practices of other religions in the area? If we read the passage this way, how might it have relevance for contemporary readers?

Given this information and these questions, how would you respond to someone who used this passage to argue for women's exclusion from teaching a mixed adult Sunday school class, reading Scripture or leading prayer in public worship, or preaching and pastoral ministry?

Exercise 16

Those Problem Passages: Church and Home

This exercise will help you ponder biblical texts that are commonly used to define women's roles in the church and at home.

How have you heard these passages used?

1 Timothy 2:8-14 (Church)
Background: This passage is from a group of books commonly known as the "pastoral letters"—1 and 2 Timothy and Jude. These books can be problematic because they take such an antagonistic view of women. Likely, these letters offer a challenge to the active leadership roles women took in the early church. Women preach, teach, prophesy, speak in tongues, and exercise spiritual gifts in the church, and the writer of the Pastoral Epistles seems unsettled by such leadership. His prescriptions for congregational behavior mirror those of the patriarchal and hierarchical household of his day.

Authorship: While these letters are traditionally attributed to Paul, most scholars believe that a later writer penned these books. Compare the style, vocabulary, themes, and ideas of 1 Timothy to 1 Corinthians (a book accepted by most biblical scholars as written by Paul) to see why scholars reject the notion of Paul's authorship of the Pastoral Epistles.

Questions

1. In 1 Timothy 2:8-14, the author lays out his standards for public behavior in the church. What restrictions does he place on women?

2. Elisabeth Schüssler Fiorenza sees in the Pastoral Epistles the stratification of church leadership around gender and age. She notes that gender and age rather than giftedness have become qualifications for leadership. Compare this passage with 1 Corinthians 12. Note that in 1 Corinthians, spiritual gifts are not distributed according to gender. What reason does the author of 1 Timothy give for restrictions on women's leadership? How does his argument compare with Paul's in Romans 5?

3. How does this author suggest women will attain salvation?

4. How does his argument compare with what the rest of the Bible teaches about salvation?

5. Many women biblical scholars argue that Jesus instituted a "discipleship of equals." The rest of Scripture attests that neither salvation nor spiritual gifts are determined by gender. The fact that this writer felt the need to limit women's leadership suggests that women had experienced the call to this discipleship of equals and were actively engaged in leading, preaching, and teaching. Yet this passage has been used throughout history to exclude women from leadership in the church.

• How do you understand this passage? Does it contribute to or diminish the full humanity of women?

• Does it restrict or further the aims of liberation?

• Do you think that the larger biblical themes of equality for women limit the relevance of this passage for contemporary women?

• What is the story behind the scenes of this letter? That is, what were women doing in the church at this time?

Ephesians 5:21–6:9 and Colossians 3:18-19 (Home)

Background and Authorship: Again, although these books purport to be written by Paul, they differ in style and substance from Paul's authentic writings. Most significantly for our purposes, we see again that these books reflect a time after Paul when women's roles had been diminished from the discipleship of equals.

These passages belong to a genre known as the *household code.* The household code prescribes behaviors for people within a family based on gender, age, and social status. The Roman household, on which these behaviors were based, was a hierarchical structure in which a number of people (women, children, slaves) were economically dependent on the master of the house who held authority over them. The early church was a movement within households, and so the pattern of households affected the pattern of the church. The early Christian movement challenged the hierarchical household pattern because it accepted converts, regardless of their status in the household and apart from the householder's participation or conversion. In this way, the early Christian movement was subversive within the Roman household hierarchy. The biblical household codes then function to restore the values of the hierarchical household within the Christian movement.

Throughout history, these household codes have been used to silence and marginalize women, both in the home and in the church. Because the household codes reflect the hierarchies of both the family home and the church home, they effectively enforce women's submission in both.

Questions

1. Do you think households today have "codes?" Do you think these codes have changed/are changing?

2. Take a look at the analogy of husbands/wives and Christ/church in the Ephesians passage. Many feminist biblical scholars would argue that the analogy fails and undercuts the argument of the author. Why do you think they might make this argument? Do you agree? Does the exhortation for men to love their wives as Christ loved the church lessen the implied inferiority of women in the exhortation for women to be subject to their husbands in everything? Again, many feminist scholars would suggest this passage plays on women's desires for love, asking women to trade their independence for love. Is it possible for men to love their wives as Christ loved the church? If not, does this argument then free women from the requirement to submit?

3. Each household code also provides exhortations to slaves. Notice that the codes assume slavery as an acceptable practice and do not seek to subvert it. Few, if any, of today's most conservative interpreters would make the argument that slavery is acceptable. What arguments do you suppose they make for this point of view, and how do they argue against a practice the Bible so readily seems to accept? Why do you think they read the sections of these passages dealing with slaves differently than they read the sections of the same passages dealing with women?

4. Just before the Ephesians household tablet, verse 21 commands, "Be subject to one another out of reverence for Christ." This passage was likely not part of the household code itself. Some scholars even suggest that the household code was a later addition to Ephesians. Go back and read Ephesians, leaving out the household code (5:22–6:9). What themes emerge? How does this reading challenge the hierarchical household outlined in the household code?

5. How do you understand the household code? Does it contribute to or diminish the full humanity of women? Does it restrict or further the aims of liberation? Why does this emphasis on hierarchy in the family and church remain so important to so many contemporary Christians?

Now that we've examined these passages about women in church and home that are often used to limit women's roles, what do you think?

Write a household code for today's home and church that recognizes the full humanity of women and furthers the aims of liberation. What would it mean to put your household code into practice?

Exercise 17

Starting Assumptions: Reading Eve against the Grain

As women, we've been taught to read the biblical text through the eyes and experiences of men. Reading against the grain means we stop and rethink how we've been taught to read the text. Instead of assuming male perspectives, we read through women's eyes and experiences. We pay attention to ways gender is at work in the text.

Questions

1. Brainstorm ways we've been taught to think about Eve. What do traditional interpretations say about her?

2. Let's consider Eve's creation. Traditional interpretation tends to rely on the account in Genesis 2, which explains that God created Eve from Adam's rib to be his helper. Look at Genesis 1:26-27, however. What does it say about the creation of humankind as male and female?

3. Why do you suppose traditional interpretation favors the second creation account over the first in relation to the creation of woman?

4. Traditional interpretation argues that Eve is created as Adam's "helper," which suggests that she is his subordinate. The Hebrew phrase here is *ezer kenegdo*, which means a partner or equal that supports, protects, and aids. Verse 18 may be better translated, "I will make [the man] an equal" or "I will make a corresponding strength or power." Elsewhere in the Bible, the word *ezer* refers to God as helper. Certainly, we would not suggest that God's role as helper to men makes God subordinate.

• Why do you think many interpreters favor understanding "helper" in reference to Eve as implying subordination?

• What are the liberatory possibilities of understanding the Hebrew word *ezer* to mean equal or corresponding in strength? How does this translation of the word challenge the notion of Eve's creation as subordinate to Adam?

5. Turn to the story of the Fall in Genesis 3. Try to put aside what you've been told about this story, and read it as if you've never read it before. What do you notice?

6. This text, perhaps more than any other, has been used to support women's subordination. Because of Eve's participation in the Fall, she is condemned to be ruled over by her husband. In this passage, we have the story of two particular people. Eve's judgment is because of her specific role in the events of the story. The text does not say that the woman brings about judgment on all humanity. Why do you think subsequent interpreters have read this as a story about all women?

7. Notice what else the text does not say:

- It does not say that Eve in any way seduced Adam to eat of the fruit.
- It does not say how Eve knew of the commandment not to eat of the fruit.
- It does not say that the serpent is evil.
- It does not say that Adam in any way tried to intervene or stop Eve (it does say that he was with her when she spoke with the serpent).
- It does not say that Eve or Adam is cursed (only the serpent is cursed).

Given that the text does not say these things, why do you think we are often given the impression that it does?

8. How might this text reflect the patriarchal cultures that created it? What biases against women are evident in this text? How has this text been harmful to women? How is gendered power expressed in this text? How might our sense of the Bible change if we ask these kinds of questions?

9. What are the liberatory possibilities of this text? How might we read Eve to discover what is positive about her? What can we learn from Eve that can be empowering for contemporary women?

Write Eve's story from her perspective. What might Eve have to say to us?

Exercise 18

Highlighting Women: In Her Own Words

One of the easiest ways to read the Bible with women in mind is simply to pay attention to the women in the text. Rather than seeing them as flat characters whose sole purpose is to move the story of the men along, we can highlight them, examine their stories, imagine the rest of the story.

In the Bible, she's not given her own name. We just know her as Job's wife. Turn to the book of Job and read chapters 1, 2, and 42. Now write her story in first person, as if she is telling it.

Questions

1. The book of Job deals with the problem of suffering. What additional issues does Job's wife raise for this theological problem? Do you think Job's story provides an adequate answer? Why or why not?

2. What have you learned from writing your version of the story? What do these readings suggest to you about the biblical story? What questions does this activity raise for you?

3. How do you tell your own stories? How do you tell your stories about suffering? About joy? Who hears your stories? What effects do your stories have on your listeners? What effects do they have on you? What roles do your stories play in your faith journey?

For further study

Betsy Sholl's "Job's Wife" from *Rooms Overhead* (Farmington ME: Alice James Books, 1986) offers a poetic perspective on how Job's wife may have felt. Find this poem online or at the library and consider the following questions: What do you think the poet is saying to us? What feelings does she attribute to Job's wife? What is Job's wife's response to God in this poem? How is this poem similar to or different from the story you wrote?

Exercise 19

Retelling the Story through Poetry

When we retell a story from the Bible, we see it in new ways. We can also use poetry to retell a story. Because poetry relies on images, rhythm, and an economy of words, it can lead us to different understandings of a story. For example, here's a poem I wrote based on the story of the woman caught in adultery:

The Woman Taken in Adultery
She bears alone their scorn,
their spit, their wrath,
their stones.
She stands alone
under the weight
of their eyes
voyeurs of sin.
She receives alone
their taunts, their sneers
self-hatred
and envy of her courage.

While he hides
under a prayer shawl
among the crowd
reciting the *shema**
and grasping a lying stone.

*The *shema* is a prayer based on Deuteronomy 6:4. In Hebrew, *shema* means "hear." Deuteronomy 6:4 begins, "Hear, O Israel."

Questions

1. What does this poem add to your understanding of the story of the woman caught in adultery?

2. How does it complicate the story?

Now it's your turn. Select a woman's story in the Bible and retell it through poetry. Then reflect on what you learn through this process.

Exercise 20

Jewish Feminist Readings of the Bible

We can also find help in our reading of the Bible by learning from Jewish feminists' readings of Scripture. Jewish feminists challenge traditional readings that exclude women. For example, they ask if women's experiences are included in the text. Take a look at the story of the Exodus. In particular, pay attention to the story of the covenant in Exodus 19 and 20. What does the story assume about the gender of "the people"—note verses 19:15 and 20:17? Jewish feminists point out the assumption that the people are the men. In the Exodus story, the women are still not liberated. Women readers must generally write themselves back into the story because, of course, they were there to receive the covenant.

Midrash is a Jewish practice of imagining the rest of the story; it tells the story beyond the story we have on the page. Feminist midrash focuses particularly on expanding the stories of women.

1. Choose a biblical story. Read it as it stands in the text. Then tell the story by including women or expanding women's roles. Imagine what the women might have felt, thought, and done if we had the entire story.

What do you learn from practicing feminist midrash? Did your story teach you something new? How might you use midrash as a way to explore other women in the Bible?

2. Read Genesis 22:1-19, a passage known in Jewish interpretation as the *akedah*, the binding of Isaac. Jewish feminist poet and scholar Alicia Ostriker sees this story as part of a larger biblical pattern of the repression of female power and agency as a condition and consequence of an exclusively male covenant. She says, from a feminist perspective, the *akedah* "represents the overthrow of matrilinearity and the binding of the sons to potentially murderous human and divine fathers." Sarah's death immediately follows the *akedah*, confirming the defeat of female power.

How do the following stories offer examples of the pattern Ostriker identifies?

i. Eve (Gen 1–2)

ii. Leah (Gen 29)

iii. Miriam (Num 12)

Ostriker calls the story of the Exodus and the promised land "disastrous" from a feminist perspective. She explains that earlier values of peace, prosperity, closeness to biological experience, and a lively relationship between husbands and wives—core values of family life—are replaced by values of nationhood, which are military, priestly, and legal. Women essentially disappear from the narrative as personalities and become objects under Jewish law. But, Ostriker argues, women's oppression is not the whole story. The Bible also invites transgressive readings, readings that challenge the dominant interpretation.

3. How can feminist midrash be a helpful tool for you as a reader of the Bible? What does doing a "transgressive" reading of the Bible mean to you? How might transgressive readings support your growth as a reflective Christian woman?

For further study

Locate two poems titled "Lot's Wife," one by Wislawa Szymborska (*Poems New and Collected 1957–1997* [London: Faber Poetry, 1999]) and one by Kristine Batey (*Introduction to Critical Reading* [Birmingham: University of Alabama, 2012]) and "The Song of Miriam" by Alicia Ostriker (Rebecca Schwartz, ed., *All the Women Followed Her* [Mountain View CA: Rikudei Miriam Press, 2001]). How are these poems feminist midrash that invite transgressive readings of the biblical text?

Exercise 21

Learning from Women in Patriarchy I

Read the story of Hagar in Genesis 16 and 21.

When read from a traditional perspective, this story is about a threat to God's promise to Abraham to become the father of the nation of Israel. In this reading, Abraham's liaison with Hagar is a sign of faithlessness, and the birth of Ishmael signals a threat to a legitimate son of Sarah's, but, if we read it as a story about the women, especially about Hagar, very different issues emerge. What stories do you imagine Hagar and Sarah might tell?

1. Describe elements of patriarchy you see in the story. How does patriarchy affect Hagar? Sarah? Is there any way out for them?

2. How do ethnic and class distinctions shape Sarah and Hagar's experiences of patriarchy?

3. Phyllis Trible, a Baptist Hebrew Bible scholar, suggests that this narrative is a story of family conflict over offspring and inheritance. How does this interpretation reflect understandings of the patriarchal culture in which the story is embedded?

4. Feminist critics have noted that often the stories of biblical mothers serve male interests. How does Sarah as a mother conform to androcentric (male-centered) interests? How do stories about mothers' androcentrism reinforce patriarchy? Can you think of other biblical stories in which motherhood functions to validate patriarchal interests? How does the story of Hagar ultimately become the story of Ishmael, just as the story of Sarah becomes the story of Isaac?

5. Womanist (black feminist) interpreters often read Hagar's story in light of the experiences of black women in slavery in the United States. How might Hagar's story compare with the stories of black slave women?

6. Feminist scholars have identified a genre of "rape narrative" in the Bible, stories about sexual violence against women. Traditionally, biblical critics did not classify these stories as stories about rape because they maintained that, in Israel's patriarchal society, women were the property of men and therefore did not have the right to consent. They claim that consent was not an issue for ancient Israelites and therefore should not be an issue for contemporary interpreters who, they say, are imposing modern perspectives onto the biblical text. How is the story of Hagar a rape narrative? What roles do gender, ethnicity, and social class play in the narrative? Do you think contemporary readers are imposing inappropriate standards on this text by labeling it a rape narrative?

In patriarchy, women are often pitted against one another, especially for male attention and male favors. Write a dialogue between Hagar and Sarah that reflects these tensions. Then, reimagine their relationship as one in which they become allies to one another as women trapped in patriarchy. Write that dialogue.

8. What do you learn from Hagar and Sarah as women in patriarchy that you can apply to your own life?

For further study

Locate "Hagar to Sarai" by Honorée Fanonne Jeffers (*Outlandish Blues* [Middletown CT: Wesleyan University Press, 2003]). What issues of gender, ethnicity, and patriarchy does Jeffers address?

Exercise 22

Learning from Women in Patriarchy II

Questions

1. In the previous exercise, we looked at the story of Hagar, Sarah, and Abraham as a story of women trapped in patriarchy. Against this narrative of patriarchy and ethnic power, however, is a counter-narrative in which God comes to Hagar and assures her. How does this counter-narrative challenge the prevailing patriarchy of the other parts of the story?

2. In the Bible, the setting of the wilderness is theologically significant. One scholar suggests that in Genesis 16, the wilderness represents temporary escape, transformation, and rite of passage for a hero. Another contends that in Genesis 21, the wilderness takes on large social and political significance as a "location outside civilization, where entire nations can live at risk with God" (Thomas B. Dozeman, "The Wilderness and Salvation History in the Hagar Story," *Journal of Biblical Literature* 117 [1998]: 32). How does the wilderness work for Hagar in her story? How does Hagar's wilderness challenge the patriarchy of Abraham's world?

3. Hagar is the first person in the Bible to encounter God, and she names God. What is the significance of the name she gives God? What is the significance of this encounter in the counter-narrative?

4. How might the traditional reading of the story that sees Hagar as a threat to God's promise to Abraham support contemporary conditions, such as the ongoing subordination of women, the sexual use of women, and the enslavement of women? In this story, God's preferential option for the oppressed seems ambiguous. God meets Hagar in the wilderness but commands her to return to her slavery. God promises safety and prosperity for Ishmael, but Hagar eventually disappears from the narrative, her importance being in her capacity to bear a son. How do these parts of the story underscore women's marginalization in the view of the writer/redactor? Do you see similar examples around you in the contemporary world? Who are today's Hagars?

5. What does Hagar's story say to contemporary women about what patriarchy means and how women must acknowledge our differences in order to support one another's struggles for justice? How does the story illustrate the traps of androcentrism for women?

6. Feminist scholars warn of the possibilities of collusion of the biblical text with present politics. Therefore, feminist readers must always ask, "Whom does this reading serve?" or "Who stands to benefit from a particular interpretation, and who is likely to be harmed by that reading?" How would you answer these questions in relation to the various readings offered in the questions above?

7. As women still living in patriarchy, how do we work together to challenge the conditions that create injustice for ourselves and women all around the world?

Exercise 23

Reading Suspiciously: Jesus and Women

Reading suspiciously means that we question the narrator; we don't accept his premises at face value. This kind of reading recognizes the patriarchal world in which these stories were told and written down and the ways these stories may have been used then (and now) to subordinate women. Read the following stories (or divide them among your group):

The Widow and Her Mite (Mark 12:41-44 and Luke 21:1-4)
The Samaritan Woman at the Well (John 4:1-49)
Mary and Martha (Luke 10: 38-42; John 11:1-45; John 12:1-11)
Mary Magdalene (Matthew 27:55-61; 28:1-10; Mark 15:40-47; 16:1-8; Luke 8:1-3; 24:1-11; John 19:25; 20:1-18)
The Hemorrhaging Woman (Matthew 9:20-22; Mark 5:24b-34; Luke 8:42-48)
The Woman Who Anointed Jesus (Matthew 26:6-13; Mark 14:3-9; Luke 7:37-50)

Questions

1. Make note of the following as you read:
    - What stories go before and after these stories
    - Why these stories may fall where they do in the longer narrative of the Gospel
    - How the story varies from Gospel to Gospel
    - Who speaks and who doesn't
    - Who is passive and who is active
    - Who is included and who is excluded
    - Who has power and who doesn't
    - Who acts and who is acted upon
    - Ways male interests are featured in the text
    - What notions of male superiority are embedded in the text
    - Ways the text subordinates or liberates women
    - Assumptions about women, men, and gender roles
    - Structures of power
    - Ways Jesus challenges or reinforces gender norms
    - Ways Jesus responds to patriarchy and expectations about male behavior
    - Ways Jesus sides with the marginalized and oppressed

2. What do these stories suggest about Jesus' relationships with women? What do they suggest about the biblical authors' views of women? How might these stories have affected women in the early church?

3. How have these stories been interpreted traditionally? Have these interpretations been used to subordinate women or reinforce stereotypes or limitations?

4. What do these stories say to you as a woman in your community?

5. What are the liberatory possibilities of these stories? Do these stories contribute to or diminish the full humanity of women?

6. Choose one of these stories and retell it, imagining it as a story about a world of justice.

7. What do liberatory readings of these stories suggest you do?

Exercise 24

Analyzing Gender Relations: Dinah

This activity will help you pay specific attention to the dynamics of gender in a biblical story. In particular, you'll look at how relationships reflect gender.

Read the story of Dinah in Genesis 34.

Questions

1. Describe the relationships between women and men in the text.

2. What gender norms are apparent in the text?

3. How are women and men valued in the text?

4. In this story, Dinah sets out on a journey. What does this suggest about her? Given what happens to her, what does the text suggest about women like Dinah?

5. Who speaks in this story, and who doesn't? What does this suggest?

6. Why are Dinah's brothers distressed?

7. Where do the narrator's sympathies seem to lie?

8. How does the narrator try to focus our attention on what he sees as the "real" issues?

9. Dinah eventually disappears from the story. What does this suggest?

10. How do the story's attitudes about women, violence, and rape continue in our time?

Phyllis Trible identifies biblical stories of abused women as "texts of terror." She says that a feminist reading of these stories functions as a memoriam to offer sympathetic readings of abused women. For her, this approach "interprets stories of outrage on behalf of their female victims in order to recover a neglected history, to remember a past that the present embodies, and to pray that these terrors shall not come to pass again" (*Texts of Terror: Literary-Feminist Readings of Biblical Narratives* [Philadelphia: Fortress Press, 1984]).

Questions

1. How can feminist readers use this text to challenge the assumptions of both the narrator and contemporary readers that justify the subordination, devaluing, or harm of women?

2. How do these stories of rape and violence against women make you feel? How do you respond to the way these stories are presented in the Bible?

3. What can we learn from these stories that applies to our contemporary situation?

Exercise 25

Reading for Structures of Power: The Woman Caught in Adultery

In this activity, you'll pay attention to structures of power and how women are situated in those structures. In patriarchy, power works to maintain male domination over women. This activity will help you develop a lens for seeing how structural power (power embodied in social institutions, such as in religion, the family, and work) and ideologies (pervasive ideas that are often assumed to be natural and inevitable) work in the biblical text.

Read the story of the woman caught in adultery in John 7:53–8:11.

Questions

1. How is power used in the text?

2. Who has power and who doesn't?

3. Who acts and who is acted upon?

4. How are structures of male power evident in the text?

5. How does Jesus challenge the structures of male power?

Some scholars suggest that reading the story to posit Jesus as a champion of women actually reinforces the structures of male power by turning Jesus into a knight in shining armor who rescues the damsel in distress. How does this understanding affirm gender roles?

Other scholars see this story as a challenge to the entire system of patriarchy. In Jesus' time, wives belonged to their husbands, and adultery was an affront to the husband's right to his property and men's right to control women's sexuality. By refusing to side with the men, Jesus refused to participate in reestablishing male honor. In fact, he gave up male honor to restore this woman's honor. He considered the woman's adultery and the sins of the men to be the same, and he confronted them both to choose a better way of living. In so doing, he offered a vision of a re-ordered social system in which both women and men could choose a new way of living. In essence, as one scholar puts it, the story suggests that men should quit proclaiming their sinlessness in relation to women and should admit their own sinful involvement with patriarchy. They should follow Jesus and break with patriarchy. This story, then, becomes an invitation to men to join in Jesus' radical social re-ordering (Elizabeth E. Green, "Making Her Case and Reading It Too: Feminist Readings of the Woman Taken in Adultery," in *Ciphers in the Sand: Interpretations of the Woman Taken in Adultery (John 7:53–8:11)*, ed. Larry J. Kreitzer and Deborah W. Rooke [Sheffield, England: Sheffield Academic Press, 2000] 263).

Another scholar points out that perhaps this woman's involvement in adultery suggests that she has accepted the patriarchal vision of herself as a sex object. By telling her to go and sin no more, Jesus is challenging her to reject patriarchy's view of women and not to see herself as a sex object any longer (Sharon Muhlenkort, "The Story of the Used Woman," *Daughters of Sarah* 13 [1987]: 13).

Questions

1. How do structures of power affect women today, especially women's sexuality? How does this reading challenge structures of power? What would it mean today for men to refuse patriarchy?

2. How have contemporary women internalized the dynamics of power represented in the text? What would it mean for women today to refuse the patriarchal vision of themselves?

3. Are there ways you have internalized patriarchal visions of women? Are there things you should do to free yourself from the limitations of internalized patriarchal visions of women?

Exercise 26

Avoiding Anti-Semitism in Reading the Bible

Many times Christians inadvertently read the Bible in ways that are anti-Semitic (discriminatory toward Jews). For examples, we have probably all heard the erroneous claim that the Jews killed Jesus (he was executed by the Romans), or we've heard Bible stories told in ways that Jews become the villains. A close reading of Scripture requires that we also pay attention to our own stereotypes or misinformation that may be clouding our reading of the text. In this particular instance, we should pay attention to a number of things to avoid an anti-Semitic reading of the Bible.

1. Be aware of the history of anti-Semitic readings of the Bible, including Christian feminist readings. Remember that

a. Jesus is himself a Jew;

b. The actors in these stories, who may or may not be Jewish, do not represent their entire group of people;

c. Jesus' teachings grow out of the Jewish history, theology, and wisdom he learned in his community; and

d. Jesus always worked within the framework of Judaism; he did not intend to start a separate religion.

2. Can you think of examples of anti-Semitic readings of the biblical text you have heard? Think of interpretations of the stories in the Gospels when Jesus happens to encounter Jewish leaders or stories in the book of Acts or Paul's writings in Romans. How could you challenge these readings?

Exercise 27

Mujerista Biblical Interpretation

In *mujerista* theology, the starting point for biblical interpretation is Latinas' experiences and struggle for survival (Ada María Isasi-Díaz, *Mujerista Theology* [Maryknoll NY: Orbis Books, 1996]). The critical lens for biblical interpretation for Latinas is liberation—both cultural and physical survival. *Mujerista* interpretation, therefore, is not concerned only with personal salvation; rather, the Bible is used to advance the struggle for liberation. In this *mujerista* interpretation, the Bible is interpreted through the lens of Latina liberation; it is authoritative only insofar as it supports Latina liberation.

Elements in Latina interpretation

1. *Need:* the Bible is used when it is needed; it is interpreted to meet daily needs for survival and liberation
2. *Struggle for liberation:* the critical lens for interpreting the Bible is its usefulness in Latinas' struggle for liberation
3. *Part of struggle for Latinas' preferred future:* the Bible must play a role in helping Latinas move toward their vision of the future. This vision of the future includes:
    a. Rejection of vision of equality within existing structures: present structures are oppressive; equality cannot be achieved in the contemporary oppressive structures
    b. Refusal to be involved in horizontal violence against other oppressed groups: liberation cannot be at the expense of someone else
    c. Praxis (a liberatory method of taking action, reflecting on that action, and taking renewed action based on reflection): it is a revolutionary act for Latinas to interpret the Bible; typically male scholars have not considered Latinas' ability to interpret the Bible or contribute to the field of biblical studies; Latina's praxis claims their right to think for themselves and define themselves
    d. Ecumenism: people and churches should work together across differences, acknowledging their common faith
    e. Reconstituting church structures, especially hierarchy and privilege: the church should be restructured to reflect and support equality and justice
    f. Rejection of split between personal and political
    g. Respect for self-determination
    h. Redefinition of power: power is not dominance but agency, collaboration, and creativity
    i. Evaluation of public policy from liberation viewpoint
    j. Goal of achieving the common good

Most Latinas know the Bible through hearing it—oral tradition rather than text. They listen and tell Bible stories. They use Bible stories to find someone in the story who will be a source of hope for them. They connect Bible stories to their stories. They use Bible stories as interpretive keys in understanding and struggling against oppression. The Bible then helps them ask questions rather than provide answers. The starting point for biblical interpretation is the situation at hand, not the Bible.

Mujerista Interpretation: The Story of Shiphrah and Puah, Exodus 1:15-22
Read the story and consider the following questions.

Questions

1. How might this story speak to the liberation of Latinas? How does this story frame God's liberating involvement in daily life?

2. How does this story refuse to pit oppressed people against one another?

3. How do Shiphrah and Puah claim the right to define themselves?

4. How do they refuse to divide the personal and political?

5. How do their actions redefine power, privilege, and hierarchy?

6. How do their actions critique public policy?

7. What might we imagine the preferred future for Shiphrah and Puah would look like?

8. How might this story speak to the lives of undocumented people in the United States?

Between 1960 and 1996, more than 100,000 Guatemalan women were raped during the brutal civil war between CIA-backed right-wing generals and left-wing insurgents. Two hundred thousand people died. Many of the women were indigenous Mayans.

9. How do you feel when you hear these stories of mass rape, torture, and genocide? What do you do with these feelings? How do you understand God's presence in these horrific events?

10. How does recognizing the context of these events help you understand the call for liberation, particularly among Latin American liberation theologians?

11. How do you imagine Shiphrah and Puah might have felt when the Pharaoh asked them to participate in genocide?

12. How might the story of Shiphrah and Puah speak to the survivors of torture?

13. From the perspective of *mujerista* interpretation, how might this story encourage Latinas in their struggle against oppression?

Exercise 28

Reading Rahab: Liberationist and Postcolonial Interpretations

Rahab is a complex character who invites multiple, competing, and often contradictory interpretations from various feminist viewpoints. As we explore these interpretations, remind yourself to think about how we hold in mind widely divergent viewpoints and learn from each of them without needing to determine that one is the only or the most correct.

Read the story of Rahab in Joshua 2 and 6:22-25.

1. Liberationist Viewpoints

Liberation theologians and biblical critics understand themes of oppression and liberation to be at the center of the biblical text. The oppressed are the poor, the powerless, the exploited, and the marginalized. For feminist liberationists, paying attention to the role of gender in oppression is essential. The good news of the Bible is that liberation is possible. God is the liberator of the oppressed, but humans have an essential role to play in actualizing liberation by restructuring oppressive social institutions, ideologies, and practices.

• How might liberationists situate Rahab as someone who is oppressed?

• How might God in this story be explained as demonstrating a "preferential option for the poor"?

• Who in the story is on God's side in this liberatory endeavor?

• Who acts on behalf of justice and in what ways?

2. Postcolonial Viewpoints

Postcolonial feminist viewpoints are concerned with the ways power, gender, and colonial concerns are deployed in the text. (Colonizing is the act of taking another's land, as well as replacing others' cultures and sense of self with those imposed by the dominating group.) In addition to critiquing colonial domination, postcolonial feminist interpretations also offer counter-readings from the perspectives of women in the "contact zone," the places of colonial encounter where people from different geographic areas come into contact with one another, often in situations of inequality and conflict. Postcolonial feminist readers also scrutinize interpretations offered by other critics for their colonial entanglements, and they emphasize the contributions of ordinary readers who offer unique perspectives from their locations as marginalized women.

• How might we read the story of Rahab from the Canaanite perspective?

• How might we evaluate the circumstances that led Rahab into prostitution?

• How might Rahab be read as a version of the Pocahontas of popular imagination?

• Musa Dube notes that in many narratives, women often represent land, and conquering women symbolizes conquering land. How does Rahab's story justify inhabiting the land of other people?

• How is Rahab herself colonized? How does she internalize the values of the colonizers?

• How does Rahab represent the intersection of colonialism and sexism?

• Dube suggests that a postcolonial feminist reading of Rahab requires creating counter-narratives. Who are the "Rahabs" who have resisted and risen up against the colonizers?

3. Look back at old Sunday school materials or popular books about the Bible or even Bible commentaries. How do they interpret Rahab? Do any of these interpretations further the goal of taking the land or replacing others' cultures with the ideas of the dominant group?

4. What do liberationist and postcolonial interpretations of Rahab suggest about the complexity of biblical characters and stories? What does Rahab's story suggest about the complexities of women's lives under patriarchy and colonialism? How is Rahab's story relevant to the lives of contemporary women? How is her story relevant to your life?

5. How might we use the story of Rahab to challenge systems that oppress and colonize?

Source: Kwok Pui-lan, "Making the Connections: Postcolonial Studies and Feminist Biblical Interpretation," *The Postcolonial Biblical Reader*, ed. R. S. Sugirtharajah (Malden MA: Blackwell Pub., 2006) 48–49.

Exercise 29

Reading for Liberation: Anna the Prophet

Read the story of Anna in Luke 2:36-38.

Questions

1. How would you describe Anna?

A group of South African women used these words to describe Anna. Would you agree?
Independent
Trustworthy
Exemplary
Empowering

2. According to the text, Anna is a prophet, living in the temple, and proclaiming good news to those seeking redemption. What do you think a prophet is? What is the prophetic role of contemporary women?

3. Anna is from a lower class and a widow. She would not normally have held much status in her society. Yet she is in a role of public leadership. What might Anna's story suggest for modern readers?

4. The South African women readers of this story saw Anna as someone who "encourages women to trust in themselves and to be trusted by other people in the community." How would this liberatory reading challenge notions that women are dependent and untrustworthy? That they should be silent and not lead?

5. How might Anna be a role model for women today?

Source: Gloria Kehilwe Plaatjie, "Toward a Post-Apartheid Black Feminist Reading of the Bible: A Case of Luke 2.36-38," in *Voices from the Margins: Interpreting the Bible in the Third World*, ed. R. S. Sugirtharajah (Maryknoll NY: Orbis, 2006) 463–483.

Exercise 30

Imagining Justice for Miriam

Read the story of Miriam in Numbers 12:1-15.

In this story, Miriam and Aaron challenge Moses' right to be the only one who speaks for God. In return, Miriam becomes leprous and is sent away in shame for seven days before God heals her.

Individual and Group Activities

1. Imagine that you are Miriam, and retell this story from your perspective as a tale of injustice and the possibilities of justice. What world of justice would Miriam dream?
2. Write a poem about this text that imagines justice for Miriam.
3. If you are studying this book in a group, role-play this story with the characters of Miriam, Aaron, Moses, and the Lord, again focusing on how the story might play out as a tale of justice for Miriam.

Questions

1. Have you faced injustice in your own life? How did you feel about that injustice?

2. What would have been needed for that moment in your life to be an experience of justice rather than injustice?

3. Can you think of other instances of injustice individual women or women as a group have faced? What is needed to create justice in these situations?

4. How can you become an instrument of justice in the world?

Exercise 31

Telling Our Stories of Learning Theology

Being a reflective Christian requires us to be thoughtful about how we have come to hold our beliefs and how those beliefs affect us and others. We learn and do theology throughout our lives. This exercise asks you to reflect on your own journey with theology. For each of the questions below, write or tell a story.

Questions

1. What are your earliest recollections of learning some theological concept?

2. When did you first become aware that something was a belief and that you had a choice to believe it or not?

3. When was the first time you realized that other people held other beliefs?

4. Was there a time when a belief you held was challenged and you changed your belief based on that challenge?

5. Was there a time when a particular theological idea became very important for you?

6. Was there a time when your belief came into conflict with the belief of a friend, family member, or your church?

7. Was there a time when a belief changed your behavior or affected your life in an important way?

8. Have your beliefs ever led you to act unkindly toward others? Have you ever been judgmental of others because of your beliefs? Have your beliefs ever made you unhappy with yourself?

9. Have your beliefs ever led you to act with compassion toward others? Have you ever been forgiving because of your beliefs? Have your beliefs ever helped you accept yourself?

10. When have you experienced doubt about your beliefs?

11. What beliefs are most important to you and why?

12. How has your journey with belief had an impact on you?

The Production of Theology

What we believe is often the product of what our church or denomination teaches us. We often fail to ask how these beliefs came to be. Theological ideas are constructions; they are created by people who struggle to understand God from their own social locations and with their own biases and agendas. That means we need to pay attention to how and why the beliefs espoused by our churches, denominations, and leaders came to be. This helps us find the gaps and identify the places where the experiences of others may have been neglected or excluded, and it helps us find the places where God can speak to us in new ways in our own times and places. Answer the questions below to begin to examine how theology has been produced in your context.

Questions

1. How is theology done in your church/denomination?

2. Who controls the creation of theology in your church/denomination? Who controls its dissemination? Who has access to this theology and who doesn't? Are there certain questions that get asked and certain questions that don't?

3. How do church/denominational structures affect the creation of theology? Are official theological stances determined by a single leader, by a group of ordained people, by a representative body, by consensus or by vote?

4. How is theology passed on in your church/denomination? Who controls the means of passing on theology?

5. Are some people systematically disadvantaged by the way theology in your church/denomination is constructed, produced, and/or taught?

6. How is the production of theology in your church/denomination affected by gender? By race? By social class? By national origin? By language?

7. How do many of the historical developments of theology in your church/denomination reflect the concerns of the dominant culture? How do they reflect the concerns of the oppressed?

8. Who benefits from the production of theology in your church/denomination? Who may be harmed by the ways theology is produced in your church/denomination?

9. What is your role in the production of theology?

Exercise 33

Wealth and Poverty: Whose Side Is God On?

This exercise will help you use the formative factors of theology to think about issues of wealth and poverty. Drawing on experience, Scripture, tradition, revelation, and culture, you can begin to think broadly about Christian views on the topic and come up with your own theology of wealth and poverty.

Questions

Experience

1. What is your experience of wealth/poverty? What experiences of wealth/poverty have you seen in/learned from books or movies? What experiences of wealth/poverty have you heard about from the rich/the poor? What do you think it is like to be very wealthy? What do you think it is like to be very poor?

2. What theological issues do those experiences raise for you? Do you wonder if God is rewarding the wealthy and punishing the poor? Do you think God draws a distinction between the deserving and undeserving?

3. If we consider the experiences of poor women who have been trafficked into sex work, how might we think about sin? How might their experiences cause us to think about suffering?

4. In Appalachia, poverty is endemic, and one of the few decent paying jobs is in the mines. Many of the young men of the region go down into the coal mines to earn their living. The coal mines do pay a living wage, but many of the workers eventually develop black lung disease. The owners of the coal mines are very wealthy and often live in mansions next to the shacks where entire families live. The coal goes to power our lights and TVs and computers, but we also know that burning coal contributes to climate change and environmental degradation. How does the reality of the coal industry in Appalachia shape our theology of wealth and poverty? What might this reality suggest about the nature of community or the shape of social justice?

5. Is suffering always redemptive? How would poverty, hunger, and disease of refugees from war-torn countries challenge us to think about sin and suffering? As most of us watched the aftermath of Hurricane Katrina, we saw that those left behind in the disaster were mostly poor and black and female. How might their experiences cause us to think about sin and suffering?

6. Most of us have heard the old adages that we should pull ourselves up by our bootstraps and that God helps those who help themselves. Still a single mother who works fulltime at a minimum wage job lives in poverty. She may not have health benefits or paid sick leave. What does her experience have to teach us? Is her plight the result of sin (hers or someone else's) or bad choices? The will of God? The consequence of oppressive systems and structures? Are we as Christians in any way responsible to her? If not, why not? If so, what is our responsibility?

7. Some Christians argue that wealth is a blessing from God in response to people's faith. Do you agree? Is all wealth a blessing from God, even if the wealthy are not Christians or have earned their wealth in less than ethical ways? Do the wealthy have a responsibility to the poor?

8. How does poverty affect women in particular? How do economic disparities have a disproportionate impact on women and children (homelessness, hunger, exposure to toxins, vulnerability to violence, etc.)?

Scripture

In the Hebrew Bible we often see that those God blesses become wealthy. Genesis 26:12-13 tells us that God blessed Isaac, and Isaac became very wealthy. The theology of Deuteronomy asserts that good things are blessings from God and bad things are punishment from God. So if someone is rich, it is because God has blessed him; if someone is poor, it is because God has punished her. The Psalmist (112:3) tells us that those who fear the Lord will have wealth and riches in their houses. In both the Hebrew Bible and Christian Testament wealthy men and women often supported the prophets and disciples. On the other hand, the prophets often take a dimmer view of wealth, seeing it as the result of exploitation. Habakkuk (2:5) says wealth is treacherous and Jeremiah (17:11) warns that those who amass wealth unjustly will lose it. The Christian Testament writers seem to share this skepticism about wealth. Jesus declares that we cannot serve both God and wealth (Matt. 6:24) and warns that it is hard for the wealthy to enter the kingdom of God (Mark 10:23). Both testaments are fairly explicit about treatment of the poor. The book of Exodus prohibits taking interest on loans to the poor (22:25) or denying justice to the poor in their lawsuits (23:6). The book of Leviticus demands that landowners leave part of the harvest for the poor to glean (19:10; 23:22), and the book of Deuteronomy commands just payment to the poor for their work (24:14-15). The Psalmist, the writer of Proverbs, and the prophets all connect a right relationship with God to right treatment of the poor. Jesus tells his followers to give their money to the poor (Matt. 19:21); he announces his anointing to bring good news to the poor (Luke 4:18); and he commends the poor as examples (the widow who gave her small offering; the poor Lazarus who lay at the gate of the rich man). James warns against showing preference for the rich over the poor (2:1-11).

1. How do you understand what the Bible says about wealth and poverty?

2. How do you reconcile the Bible's varying views on wealth and poverty?

3. What does your understanding of the Bible's messages about wealth and poverty mean for you personally? How can you apply what you've learned?

Tradition

Many of the church fathers argued against wealth as a Christian value. Cyprian called the wealthy not masters of their money but its slaves. Ambrose, Basil, and John Chrysostom all argued that the riches of the wealthy truly belonged to the poor.[1] Mystics like Hildegard of Bingen and Julian of Norwich worked on behalf of the poor. The Catholic Church, the National Council of Churches, and a number of Protestant denominations have issued statements calling for economic justice for the poor.

The following quotation comes from John Calvin's commentary on Isaiah 58. How do you understand Calvin's reading of the text in relation to wealth and poverty?

> He goes on to describe the duties of love of our neighbor, which he had described briefly in the preceding verse; for, having formerly said that we must abstain from every act of injustice, he now shows that we ought to exercise kindness towards the wretched, and those who need our assistance. Uprightness and righteousness are divided into two parts; first, that we should injure nobody; and secondly, that we should bestow our wealth and abundance on the poor and needy. And these two ought to be joined together; for it is not enough to abstain from acts of injustice, if thou refuse thy assistance to the needy; nor will it be of much avail to render thine aid to the needy, if at the same time thou rob some of that which thou bestowest on others. Thou must not relieve thy neighbors by plunder or theft; and if thou hast committed any act of injustice, or cruelty, or extortion, thou must not, by a pretended compensation, call on God to receive a share of the plunder. These two parts, therefore, must be held together, provided only that we have our love of our neighbor approved and accepted by God.
>
> By commanding them to "break bread to the hungry," he intended to take away every excuse from covetous and greedy men, who allege that they have a right to keep possession of that which is their own. "This is mine, and therefore I may keep it for myself. Why should I make common property of that which God has given me?" He replies, "It is indeed thine, but on this condition, that thou share it with the hungry and thirsty, not that thou eat it thyself alone." And indeed this is the dictate of common sense, that the hungry are deprived of their just right, if their hunger is not relieved. That sad spectacle extorts compassion even from the cruel and barbarous. He next enumerates various kinds, which commonly bend hearts of iron to συμπάθειαν fellowfeeling or compassion; that the savage disposition of those who are not moved by feeling for a brother's poverty and necessity may be the less excusable. (*John Calvin's Commentaries On Isaiah 49–66*, Extended Annotated Edition [Altenmünster, Germany: Jazzybee Verlag, 2012] np)

Revelation

1. We've looked at Scripture, but how might the other modes of revelation affect our theologizing about wealth and poverty? How, for example, are human beings affected when they live in poverty? What happens to human nature when basic needs are not met? What happens to the natural world when it is exploited for financial gain?

2. What does history reveal to us about wealth and poverty? In particular, what does history reveal about what happens to poor women and children?

Culture

1. What are American cultural understandings of wealth and poverty? How have those understandings changed over time?

2. How have our cultural understandings of wealth and poverty affected our theological understandings?

3. For some Christians, the cultural ideas of American capitalism lead them to believe that capitalism is God's economic system. Other Christians believe capitalism is inherently harmful because it rests on the exploitation of the poor and working class. How might other cultures' understandings and experiences of wealth and poverty inform theology?

4. Many feminists argue that capitalism, as a tool of patriarchy, reinforces the subordinate status of women and ensures ongoing poverty, suffering, discrimination, and death for women. What do you think?

Now use these formative factors to think theologically about other issues such as HIV/AIDS, sexuality, or the environment.

Given all of these formative factors in theology, how would you summarize your own theology of wealth and poverty?

Note

1. See http://bramboniusinenglish.wordpress.com/2012/08/31/teachings-of-the-early-church-fathers-on-poverty-wealth/.

Exercise 34

A Biblical Theology of God

A biblical theology uses all of Scripture to develop an overarching understanding of a particular idea—in this case, God. In doing biblical theology, you'll find that Scripture doesn't always speak in one voice, but across the diversity of voices you can find unity in a commitment to faith and an ongoing encounter with God. With this approach, contradictory views can stand side by side unresolved because faith is not dependent on certainty about ideas but rather on engagement in relationship with God. The biblical text is so rich that more than one interpretation is necessary to begin to capture what is in Scripture.

The tasks of biblical theology are

- to understand the biblical text on its own terms and in its historical context, using the tools of historical criticism, and examining the issue across the entire scope of the Bible.
- to recognize the influence of one's own culture/social location on the reading of the text.
- to recognize the ways God speaks through the text.

Biblical theology is a dialogue between the text, the reader, and God. The goal of biblical theology is to involve people in both the historical witness of the text and the contemporary address of God.

Questions

1. How does the Pentateuch understand God? The Prophets? The Writings? The Gospels? Paul's Letters? The General Letters?

2. How does the Bible address immanence/transcendence? Justice/mercy? Vulnerability/immutability?

3. What descriptors does the Bible use for God?

4. What metaphors does the Bible use for God?

5. How is God active in human history throughout the Bible?

6. What overall understandings of God emerge from this process? Are there contradictory understandings?

7. Where do these understandings intersect your experiences and understandings? How does God speak to you through these understandings?

Exercise 35

Doing Narrative Theology

In narrative theology, the story is the theology. In other words, religiously significant stories express an encounter with God. The expression of this encounter in story offers us a different kind of knowing than more abstract theologies. The stories are not simply illustrations of a particular theological idea; rather, they are an expression of it. Therefore stories and other forms of theology should be in dialogue, each contributing to the theological conversation.

Four types of religiously significant personal stories are common:

1. Self-discovery stories. In these stories, you discover something about yourself and about God.

a. Write a story about a time when something profound or religiously significant happened to you.

b. Where do you see God at work in your story?

c. What do you learn about yourself in your story?

d. What do you learn about the world in your story?

2. Mystical stories. These stories express an experience of heightened awareness of the Divine.

a. Write a story about a time when you experienced a heightened awareness of Mystery.

b. What did you learn about God and yourself in your story?

c. What did you learn about the meaning of relationship with God, self, and others in your story?

3. Revelatory stories. These stories provide a moment of insight.

   a. Write a story about a time when you experienced a moment of insight.

b. What difference did that moment make for you? How did you understand things differently? How did you act differently?

4. Conversion stories. These stories are about change, about a turnaround.

   a. Write a story about a time when you changed significantly.

b. What did this change mean for you?

c. What did this change teach you about God, yourself, and others?

Questions

1. What do your personal stories suggest to you about the nature of God, about how God works in the world, and about what it means to be a human and a Christian?

2. How do your stories fit in the larger context of the Christ story and the story of Christianity itself?

3. Do your stories affirm traditional doctrinal constructions? Or do they offer challenges to the usual way of thinking about things? What happens when your personal stories run up against conventional ways of thinking about faith? How do you resolve the tension?

For further study

Fictional stories also can provide us with important insights and theological ideas. Read a story by Flannery O'Connor, such as "Revelation" or *Wise Blood.* What do these stories suggest about human nature, sin, and redemption?

Sources: William J. Bausch, *Storytelling: Imagination and Faith* (Mystic CT: Twenty-Third Publications, 1984); John Shea, *An Experience Named Spirit* (Chicago: Thomas More, 1983).

Exercise 36

Practical Theology: A Checklist for How Well My Church Is Embracing Difference

Practical theology has to do with how we put our theology into practice. In this activity, you'll examine a list of some things churches can do to embody a theology of inclusion and welcome. See how well your church does.

Use a checkmark to indicate which of the following can be found at your church.

___American sign language interpretation

___Inclusive language

___Braille hymnals

___Wheelchair ramps

___Representations of diverse people in publications

___Elevators

___Braille signs

___Outreach to teens

___Accessible bathrooms

___A stated commitment to diversity

___Large-print bulletins

___Large-print Bibles

___Addiction support groups

___Large-print hymnals

___Culturally inclusive educational materials

___Seating for wheelchairs

___Representations of diverse people in artwork

___Sound amplification

___Support for the sick and grieving

___Procedures for dealing with bias incidents

___Clothes closet

___Active recruitment of diverse members

___Soup kitchen

___Celebration of events important to diverse groups (Black History Month, Women's History Month, etc.)

___Support for community/neighborhood events

___Membership in organizations that support diversity

___Active recruitment of diverse staff members

___Invitations to diverse speakers

Questions

1. How well does your church do?

2. Do you think these items are important as a way for a church to reflect its theology?

3. Are there items on the list that make you uncomfortable or that you think don't belong? What other items should be on the list?

4. Why is reflecting our theology in our church practices important? Where is there room for improvement in your church?

Exercise 37

Practical Theology in Our Community and in Our World

Get a copy of today's local newspaper. Identify one local problem that your faith community could address.

Questions

1. What is the nature of the problem? How would you describe the problem, its causes and effects?

2. Have you previously seen similar issues in your community? What happened then? Were your/your church involved in the solution? What lessons were learned?

3. What theological issues does the problem raise—questions about human nature, the role of God in the world, sin, suffering, the environment, social justice, etc?

4. What theological responses could you/your church offer to the issue?

5. What actions could your church take to address the problem, alleviate suffering, bring about improved conditions, etc? How would these actions reflect your/your church's theology? What difference do you think these actions would make?

Now, go back to your newspaper and choose a national or global problem and answer the questions above in relation to this issue.

How do you feel about applying theology to real life issues? Sometimes we can feel overwhelmed by the enormity of the problems the world faces, and we wonder what our small contributions can do. Even the smallest of contributions does make a difference, even if it's only in the life of one individual. And taken together, our small contributions add up to much larger contributions. Imagine that you want to encourage yourself to take action.

Write an inspirational speech for yourself. Then read it to yourself in a mirror. If you are part of a group reading this book, write an inspirational speech for your group and then give it to the group.

Exercise 38

Doing Christology

Christology is the study of the person and nature of Jesus. It is an interpretation of the nature of the Christ.

Think about the pictures of Jesus you saw as a child in Sunday school or in an illustrated Bible. What did that Jesus look like? Go online and search for pictures of Jesus. You'll find pictures that reflect a variety of cultures. You may even find pictures of a female Jesus. Why do you think artists depict Jesus in such a variety of ways? What do you think of these depictions? What do they suggest about the person and nature of Jesus? Now consider these questions about Jesus.

1. What do we mean by "Christ?"

2. What is the relationship of the historical Jesus to the Christ?

3. What do we mean when we say that Jesus is fully human and fully divine?

4. Since Jesus was male, if we argue that Jesus was fully human, do we negate the place of women in the fullness of humanity?

5. If we argue that Jesus was fully human, does the embodiment of Christ give value to the body, the senses, and human relationships? What does the embodiment of Christ mean for how we understand all parts of the created world?

6. What is the work of Christ? Is Christ's redeeming work only for individual, spiritual salvation? Or does Christ's redeeming work include the present social and political liberation of all people?

7. What does the suffering of Christ mean for us, particularly as women? Does Christ's suffering mean that Christ is the one who suffers with us in our suffering? Is suffering expected and inevitable? Is suffering the consequence of evil? Must women accept their suffering? How could they challenge it as a form of sin against women?

8. What does it mean to envision Christ as the liberator of women?

9. In Korean feminist theology, Jesus is the shaman who releases the *han* (unjust suffering) of women. For many feminists, Jesus is Christ-Sophia (the Hebrew embodiment of Wisdom and a feminine name). Who is Jesus to you?

Exercise 39

Gendered Theology

Gender is something we do. That may surprise you. You probably think of gender as something we have. In reality, gender is created by the cultures in which we live. Gender teaches us how to behave, and we learn these lessons so early and so thoroughly that we think and feel that gender is something natural, inherent, and inevitable. It's really something we learn to perform based on what society tells us people with our particular body parts are supposed to be and do.

1. Think about ways you're performing gender right now. Are you wearing makeup? How is your hair styled? What clothes are you wearing? What areas did you shave this morning? What side are your buttons and zippers on? How are you sitting? What kind of jewelry are you wearing? All of these are ways we perform gender—ways we act like women or men.

2. Doing theology is also a gendered performance. Think about who gets to do and teach theology. Think about the ways the gender of the person doing the theology affects the theology that's produced. Do you think a group of women would likely have decided that the best (and often only) metaphors for God are Father, King, and Master? Might women have imagined God in other ways that could have influenced the church differently?

3. Think about how the church is organized. How is it gendered? Who does what? Who is excluded from doing what? Who wears what? Who's up front and in what capacities? As we watch what goes on in church, how does the church teach us to perform gender? How does the repetition of these gendered performances maintain gender as a notion that structures everyday behavior, social patterns, and the church itself?

4. Take a look at your church's educational literature for children. How is gender embedded in it? Look at the pictures. Who is active? Who is passive? What are people of different genders doing? What are they wearing? Read the text. What does it assume about girls and boys? What about the literature for adolescents and adults?

Sexism is the system of oppression that maintains male dominance over women. Gender plays a role in maintaining sexism by teaching women and men behaviors that repeat the gendered patterns of male dominance and female subordination. (For example, women are taught to be quiet and nice; men are taught to be assertive and speak up. The result is that men speak over women; women who are assertive are labeled with negative words; men negotiate better salaries; women experience sexual assault or domestic violence and believe or are told it is their fault.)

Despite the advances women have made, sexism persists. Here are some examples: men still make more money than women for doing the same job; women still do more of the work of the home, even if they are primary breadwinners; despite Title IX, most women's college sports programs are funded at lower levels than men's, and their events are attended less; few women are in Congress or are CEOs of Fortune 500 companies.

1. What are examples of sexism in individual and institutional beliefs, behaviors, and uses of language in the church?

2. What church policies advance sexism? What policies advance equality and justice?

3. How does sexism affect women and men in the church?

4. Many feminist theologians consider sexism to be a sin of the church. What do you think of this? If sexism is a sin of the church, what would repentance look like?

5. What would a truly egalitarian church look like?

Exercise 40

Doing a Postcolonial Feminist Theology of Church

How we think about church has been largely defined by men throughout history. Feminist theology asks us to think about the church with women at the center and to include the diversity of women in our thinking. Postcolonial feminist theology challenges us to include questions of the effects of colonization and empire on women as we think about the nature and function of the church. Think about what you already know about church from your own experiences as you answer the questions below. Then do some research to learn more about the church's involvement in colonization or the responses of women from the Two-Thirds World to the church.

Key Questions of Traditional Ecclesiology (the doctrine of the church)

1. What is the church?

2. What is the role of the church?

3. How is the church organized/governed?

4. What are the sacraments/ordinances of the church?

5. How is ecclesiology connected to Christology and soteriology (the doctrine of salvation)?

6. How has ecclesiology been expressed in church history?

Questions of Feminist Ecclesiology

1. Where are women in the church?

2. How does gender function in the church?

3. What is the mission of the church in relation to women?

4. What does the church as the "body of Christ" mean for women?

5. What are the implications of a clergy/laity duality?

6. How has the church maintained the subordination of women?

7. How has the church maintained the ideology of patriarchy?

8. What do the experiences of women say to the development of ecclesiology?

9. What can the church offer women? What can women offer the church?

10. What is the effect of the church's liturgy on women?

11. What is the significance of the gospel for women in the church?

12. What ecclesiology will promote the liberation of women?

13. Does redemption for women come within the church?

14. How do race/ethnicity, social class, sexual identity, age, and ability intersect with gender in ecclesiology? Go back through the above list of questions and ask each question again, this time for "women" substitute "black women," "Asian women," "Latinas," "Native American women," "poor women," "women with HIV/AIDS," "disabled women," "old women."

Questions of Postcolonial Feminist Ecclesiology

1. How has empire (the taking of other people's lands and resources) affected the development of the church?

2. How does the dominance of Western perspectives in theology affect ecclesiology?

3. How has the church spread empire and subordinated entire groups of people?

4. What is the church's responsibility in de-colonizing (undoing the effects of colonization)?

5. What is the meaning of justice in the church?

6. What stories do Two-thirds World women tell about church?

7. What folk wisdom, parables, proverbs, and stories about church arise from the women of the Two-thirds World?

8. Mercy Amba Oduyoye calls the church the "household of God" in which all are welcome. She adds that the church's mission, however, is to be in the world caring for those who need it and confronting injustice wherever it exists. The task of the church, she says, is to work for the well-being of the world (*Introducing African Women's Theology* [Cleveland: Pilgrim Press, 2001] 88–89). How does this image of church challenge dominant notions of church? How does it challenge the participation of the church in activities that subordinate groups of people? How does the idea of the church as the household of God make you feel? What would it mean for you for the church to be the household of God?

Exercise 41

Critiquing Traditional Theology

The theology most of us learned in church came to us as neutral, objective truth. We did not assume that the social location of those who had the power to develop Christian theology had deeply affected that theology. We didn't realize that we had never bothered to question how the maleness or whiteness or social, economic, political, and ecclesial power of theologians shaped what we took as enduring truth. Fortunately, people of color, women, people from the Two-Thirds world, and others began to challenge traditional theological assumptions and bring their perspectives to bear on theology, offering us a richer, more inclusive path to experiencing and understanding God.

Let's take a look at some traditional theological ideas and explore the perspectives they represent and the problems they create for those who are not part of the dominant paradigm (white, male, economically advantaged, able-bodied, etc.).

Critique 1: Traditional theology is rooted in men's experiences.
As theologian Elizabeth Johnson notes, men in power created images of God that, not surprisingly, look like men in power. As men exercised power in the church, they took their own privileged positions and used them to develop models for God. So God came to look more like a man in power than, say, a nurturing mother or a compassionate friend. Johnson says the result was an almost universal depiction of God as male—from the language of the liturgy to representations in art.

1. What images of God as a man in power are common in the language and practices of your church? What about in the popular imagination?

2. If we imagined God from diverse women's perspectives, what language, images, and practices might emerge?

Critique 2: Theology has set up false dualisms that make the male experience the norm.
The idea of a strict dualism between women and men is actually a Greek philosophical idea. As Johnson explains, it begins in biological differences, assigns traits based on these differences, and ends by determining social roles based on these traits. Men, then, were considered to be active, strong, and rational. Women, by contrast, were passive, weak, and emotional. Because God was identified with the male, God also became active, strong, and rational. This, in turn, justified men's dominance over women—because men are more like God, men rule over women.

Complementarianism has become increasingly popular among evangelicals. This notion argues that while women and men are of equal worth, they are assigned different roles by God based on gender. These roles align closely with traditional white twentieth-century American ideals—men are the breadwinners; women are responsible for caring for the home and raising the children; men make the decisions in the family; women submit.

1. What if we could think of God as nurturing *and* powerful, rational *and* emotional? What if we thought of humans, both men and women, as being capable of expressing the full range of human thought, emotion, and experience?

2. What if we rejected the dualism that assigns men and women traits and social roles? How would this challenge complementarianism?

3. What alternatives could we suggest if we reimagined the nature of God, the nature of humans, and the nature of family?

Critique 3: Theology has been an academic and intellectual endeavor, not accessible to the majority of people.

Very often, theology has been written by highly educated, elite academics. Often their books and articles are not accessible to the majority of the world's people, and often their theologizing is far removed from the everyday problems of poverty, violence, hunger, and abuse.

1. What do you think are the consequences of having most theology done by and for academics, especially since most of those academics are white, male, and western?

2. What challenges might the voices of the poor offer to traditional theology? If we remember that the majority of the world's poor are women and children, how might that change the critique?

3. How might theology look different if it was done by the poor? By women who have survived domestic violence? By people living with HIV/AIDS?

4. If God is the One Who Liberates, how should theology be done in order to effect liberation?

Critique 4: Theology has relegated women to second-class status.

The reformer Martin Luther wrote that women's reason for existence was to be wife and mother. In fact, he suggested that if a woman died in childbearing, it was no great loss because she died doing what she was supposed to do. He blamed Eve for the Fall and women for leading men into error. John Calvin described women as inferior to men and called them an "appendage" to men. He wrote that women were to render obedience to men.

1. How have these theological notions shaped contemporary views of women?

2. What do they suggest about the valuing of women?

A 2011 Gallup survey found that twice as many Americans would rather have a son than a daughter. Research shows that hiring practices still favor men over women, and men still make more money than women for doing the same work. What does this research suggest about our valuing of women and men?

Critique 5: Theology has excluded women from full participation in home, society, and church.

1. In what ways do women experience discrimination in the church, the home, and society?

2. How does traditional theology support discrimination? How do traditional images of God as a powerful male support discrimination? How do traditional notions of Eve and women as temptresses support discrimination? How do traditional notions of suffering, service, and sacrifice support discrimination?

3. Complementarianism argues that women and men are of equal worth and assignsk women to subordinate statuses in the home and church. Can women be both equal and subordinate?

4. Despite decades of progress in many realms, women still do more work raising children and caring for the home than do men. They also still make lower wages working the same jobs. How do you think traditional theological notions have played a role in maintaining women in these positions?

5. What other issues can you identify in which women still face discrimination and second-class status?

6. How might an egalitarian theology challenge these issues? What alternative visions could an egalitarian theology offer?

Critique 6: Theology has created stereotypes to which both women and men must conform. Fill in the chart below with stereotypes about women and men. Put an asterisk by the ones you think are supported by traditional theology. I've given you a few examples to get you started.

Men	**Women**
Rational	Emotional
Active	Passive
Breadwinner	Temptress
____________________	____________________
____________________	____________________
____________________	____________________
____________________	____________________
____________________	____________________
____________________	____________________

1. How do you think these stereotypes affect women and men and their relationships to one another?

2. What effects do they have in society? In the church?

3. How do they help maintain male dominance and female subordination?

4. How do they limit both women's and men's ability to express their full humanity? How does this limitation harm the family, the church, and society?

Critique 7: Theology has supported conquest and colonialism in the name of God.

Across the centuries, many Christian people have used theology as a justification to take the lands and resources of other people. Claiming a moral and spiritual superiority, usually based on skin color and cultural practices, these people have conquered continents, committed genocide, and stripped other peoples of their resources. Sometimes, even well-meaning and compassionate people have participated in missionizing activities that have had the same end result—entire groups of people have lost their land, resources, cultural practices, and identities because a certain theology has presumed the superiority of the conquering (white, western) people.

1. What is the legacy of colonization? What events do we see in contemporary life that reflect the ongoing effects of colonization?

2. How/where is colonization still occurring?

3. How might theology speak to the legacy of colonization and to ongoing colonization?

For further study

Using information available at the library or online, find out what roles theology and the church played in the following:

- Settlement by Europeans of what is now the United States
- Conquest of Middle Eastern lands
- Colonization of African nations

As we offer these critiques of traditional theology, we see that, when taken alone, traditional theology cannot encompass the experiences of women, people of color, people of the Two-Thirds world, the poor, those with disabilities, and others who live on the margins. We see clearly that other perspectives and skills are needed to offer a more inclusive and encompassing theology.

1. What have you learned from these critiques of traditional theology?

2. How might you apply these critiques to particular traditional formulations of theological ideas, such as sin, atonement, sanctification, and eschatology?

Source: Elizabeth Johnson, *Quest for the Living God: Mapping Frontiers in the Theology of God* (New York: Continuum, 2007) 98.

Exercise 42

Social Location and Christology

Recall the earlier activity in which you identified your social location (Exercise 2). Social location affects how we do theology. Who we are, where we live, the language we speak, and the experiences we have influence how we think about God and other important theological issues. Most theology has been done from male perspectives and assumed to apply to all people. Therefore, most theology ignores women's issues. Women theologians, however, have brought not just a gender lens but also an intersectional lens to theological issues. From their social locations, they have developed theologies that speak to the specifics of their own situations. Below are several brief summaries of how women theologians from various social locations think about Christ.

A Womanist Christ

Womanist theologians, reflecting their experience of the intersection of race and gender, envision Christ as a black female. Set against the backdrop of the history of black slavery in the United States, womanists understand Christ as the one who shares in their sufferings as black women and who is the healer who will bring about the end of their suffering. Rather than calling for an identification with and glorification of suffering, womanists encourage black women to see Christ as the liberator who calls them to believe that they deserve better and to love themselves as black women in a racist world that teaches them to hate themselves.

A Latina Christ

The thinking of Latina theologians begins in the everyday experiences of poverty, sexism, and violence experienced by Latin American women. In this context, Christ is not simply the one who liberates from sin; rather, Christ demands liberation from the social, political, and economic circumstances that keep most of the world's women in poverty. The Latina Christ also calls for the liberation of the female body that has been controlled by patriarchal cultures and a patriarchal church.

A Korean Christ

In *minjung* theology, *han* is the feeling of resentment and helplessness brought on by unjust suffering experienced by the oppressed. For the oppressed to be healed, *han* must be released. Women have their own unique and deeper *han* created by their additional experiences of suffering as women. In traditional Korean thought, *han* is released through a ceremony (*han-pu-ri*) that is conducted by shamans (usually women) and that gives voice to their suffering. For Korean Christian women, Christ is the shaman who releases *han*. Rather than "son of God," Jesus is the "big sister," like the shaman, who heals them.

An African Christ

For African women, the suffering of Christ means that Christ can be a companion in their suffering. African women, however, understand suffering not as an end in itself but as birth pangs that lead to something new. An African Christ is a midwife of a new birth. This birth, however, is not only a spiritual one but also a social, political, and economic one that addresses the conditions that create suffering for African women. The retelling of the Jesus story encourages African women to see themselves as people who can become agents in social transformation.

A Fat Christ

Many North American and British women are unhappy with their bodies. They have been taught that women's primary value is in their appearance and that beauty requires a thin body. Even religious organizations bombard them with the message that thinness is godlier and weight is the consequence of sin (overeating and lack of self-control). Traditional theology has long devalued the body—and because women are associated with the body, it has also devalued women. Theologian Lisa Isherwood explains that we need a Fat Christ who redeems the body and welcomes women in all their fleshiness.

Your Christ

Now, thinking about your own social location, who is Christ to you? How does Christ speak to your gender, race, nation, age, social class, sexual identity, ability/disability, age? How does Christ effect redemption in your life? What does Christ expect of you? How might your understanding of Christ also be limited by your social location? What can you learn from women in other social locations that can help expand your understanding of Christ?

Exercise 43

Social Class and Theology

In the United States, we often imagine ourselves as a classless society. In reality, this assumption masks the real class differences that have a tremendous impact on all of us. Other myths include the following:

- Practically everyone in the US is middle class.
- Privilege is earned.
- Everyone can move up if she or he wants.
- Everyone wants to move up.
- Class is defined by income.

In reality, the gap between the very rich and the rest of us is growing. The top 1 percent owns more wealth than the entire bottom 90 percent. Race and gender affect social class, apart from effort, education, and experience. People in the middle class own little wealth. In reality, they live from paycheck to paycheck. Most of the nation's poor are women and children. Because of the myths of class in the US, however, we assume that wealth is based on merit and that privilege is earned by hard work. Nonetheless, hard-working minimum wage earners still often live in poverty and are unable to access resources (such as education) that would allow them to earn more.

You may not think that social class has much to do with theology. But remember that most traditional theology has been developed by men who have had access to education and economic stability. Let's think about how social class has affected theology.

For example, some theologies teach that people are poor as a consequence of their bad choices or laziness. Some churches teach that God wants people to be wealthy. Some teach that wealth is a sign of God's blessing.

1. Identify ways you see that assumptions about social class have affected theology and the practices of the church.

2. Theologies of liberation, however, argue that God shows a "preferential option" for the poor. In other words, God sides with the poor and oppressed against the powerful and wealthy who oppress them. How would this theological argument address the myths of social class? How would it challenge traditional theologies? How would it challenge practices of the church? What would it suggest churches should do?

3. Unfortunately, many liberation theologies were done by men who left women out of the equation. They assumed a universal human experience of poverty and oppression that ignored how gender shapes the experience of poverty. Since women and children are the majority of the world's poor, how should theologies of liberation take account of gender? What would a liberation theology that paid attention to gender suggest the church should do?

African feminist theologian Mercy Amba Oduyoye (*Introducing African Women's Theology* [Cleveland: Pilgrim Press, 2001] 37–38) points to the significant role of reproduction in most women's lives. She notes that for most African women simply surviving pregnancy and having a live birth is a feat of overcoming poverty and oppression. Therefore, she says African women's primary resource in struggle for survival and liberation is hope. She says mothering, then, is an important metaphor for all Christians—both women and men. Mothering, she says, is all of the nurture, mentoring, and life-giving that people do and is an obligation for all people.

What do you think of Oduyoye's argument? How would our theologies look if we put hope and mothering at the center? What have been your own experiences of hope and mothering? How have those experiences shaped your thinking about God and human beings? What actions should we take in the world to embody these notions of hope and mothering?

Exercise 44

Exploring New Metaphors for God

Metaphors are images drawn from familiar human experiences and then used in fresh ways to help us explore realities that are not accessible to our everyday experience. All language about Deity is metaphorical because no one image or analogy can capture the essence of Deity.

Throughout Jewish and Christian faith communities' history, they have variously imaged Deity as Father, Shepherd, King, and Master. Originally, these metaphors helped people explore and grapple with different aspects of the nature of Deity. Many contemporary theologians, however, suggest that we need to create new, shocking metaphors for Deity that will cause us to think in new ways. Theologian Sallie McFague contends, "The best metaphors always give both a shock and a shock of recognition" (*Models of God* [Minneapolis: Fortress Press, 1987]).

In powerful metaphors, we see something about reality, and we see it in new ways.

Philosopher Alfred North Whitehead suggests that we are often plagued by what he calls the "fallacy of misplaced concreteness" (*Process and Reality* [New York: Simon & Schuster, 2010] 18). By this, Whitehead means that sometimes we make our metaphors literal. For example, instead of thinking of God as Father, we begin to think God *is* Father.

Questions

1. Why do you think the fallacy of misplaced concreteness is problematic when thinking about Deity?

2. What are some of the metaphors for Deity with which you are familiar? In what ways have those metaphors been helpful? In what ways are those metaphors limiting?

3. What are some of the metaphors for Deity that you think have fallen victim to the fallacy of misplaced concreteness?

4. What do you perceive as the consequences of taking these metaphors literally? Are there some metaphors that you think have outlived their usefulness?

5. Below are several new metaphors for Deity that are used in current theological discussion. How do you react to these metaphors? How do they make you feel? In what new ways do they cause you to think about Deity? What new ideas about the nature of Deity do they suggest to you? In what ways do they call you to reappraise your images of Deity?

a. God as Mother

b. God as Lover

c. God as Companion

d. God as Gambler

e. The earth as God's body

6. Can you think of any new "shocking" metaphors that help you think about Deity in new ways?

For further study

Locate the text of "Bring Many Names," a hymn text by Brian Wren. What does it suggest about how we understand God? How do these metaphors stretch our understandings and help us experience God in different ways?

Exercise 45

Examining Church Documents: What Do They Say about Our Beliefs?

The written documents of our churches, from the church budget to the hymnal, are theological documents. Implicit in these documents are the beliefs of those who create and subscribe to them. Not surprisingly, these documents also tell us a lot about what various groups think about women.

Questions

1. Start with your church's creed or confessional statement. What beliefs are most important in it? How are women reflected in it? What language does it use to name and describe God?

2. Now pick up your church's hymnal. What do the hymns tell you about the nature of God? Of salvation? Of the church? What do they tell you about women? Does the language of the hymnal include women? What language does it use to name and describe God?

3. Look at your church's constitution. What does its language reflect about the nature of God, salvation, the church, and humanity? How are women reflected in the document? What language does it use to name and describe God?

4. Look at your Sunday school materials. How is God represented? How are women represented?

5. Taken together, what do these documents suggest about women? Do these documents account for differences among women—across race, social class, ability, and age?

6. How does power work in these documents? Who holds power and who doesn't?

7. Who wrote these documents? Who had input and who didn't? Whose interests do these documents serve? What might that suggest?

8. Do you think these documents empower or disempower women?

9. Are there alternative documents and different voices? What do they add to the conversation?

10. How have these documents been important to you? Have they shaped you in particular ways? What do they mean to you? What role have they played in the development of your own theology?

Exercise 46

A Hopeful Utopian Vision

Mujerista theologian Ada María Isasi-Díaz calls for a *proyecto histórico* or "hopeful utopian vision" ("Burlando al Opresor: Mocking/Tricking the Oppressor: Dreams and Hopes of Hispanas/Latinas and Mujeristas," *Theological Studies* 65 [2004]: 349). She says that envisioning a utopia helps us identify needs and focus our efforts to move us toward that vision. This utopia is not impossible, she says. It must be feasible, because that is what allows us to move toward its realization. In mujerista theology, this utopia is defined by Latinas for their own liberation.

Again, start with your social location. Imagine your own hopeful utopian vision.

Questions

1. Identify both the problems you face and the problems you see in the world. Since theology begins in everyday life, what do these problems suggest about the nature of God, humanity, redemption, the church?

2. Imagine your utopia. What would it be like for you? For others? How does your utopia take into account others from different social locations? What is the role of theology in the way you have imagined your utopia?

3. What would it take to move from the world as it is to the world you envision?

4. What is the role of theology in your utopian vision? Where does God fit in? What is sin? What is redemption? What is the role of Christ? What is the role of the church? What are you called to do?

5. What concrete steps can be taken to begin moving from the current world to your utopian world?

Exercise 47

Fat Jesus: Developing a Theology of the Female Body

Feminist theologian Lisa Isherwood has developed the image of the Fat Jesus as a way to reimagine the female body. Because of women's association with the body and the devaluing of the body in patriarchal culture, women mostly feel bad about their bodies and about themselves. A feminist theology of the body reconstructs the female body in positive ways and values women as embodied humans.

Questions

1. What is your experience of your body? How would you describe it? How do you feel about it? What messages have you received about female bodies in general and your body in particular? What has the church told you about bodies?

2. In traditional theology, God is imaged as male. Philosopher Mary Daly has said that if God is male, then the male is God. By this, she means that if we only imagine God as male, then men are able to claim a greater likeness to God that gives them the right to rule over women. How might imagining God as female challenge the assumed superiority of male bodies over female bodies? How might imagining God as female suggest changes men should make in their behavior toward women? God is also typically imagined as white. What would imaging God as black, American Indian, Asian, Arab, or Latina suggest about our valuing of the wide range of human bodies?

3. Read the creation story in Genesis 2. What does it suggest about the material world? About bodies?

4. Read the Song of Songs. What does this love poem suggest about bodies?

5. Look at the stories about when Jesus touched someone or someone touched Jesus. What do they suggest about bodies?
a. Matt 8:1-3
b. Matt 8:14-15
c. Matt 9:18-19, 23-25
d. Matt 9:20-22
e. Matt 9:27-31
f. Matt 20:30-34
g. Mark 1:40-42
h. Mark 6:54-46
i. Mark 7:32-37
j. Mark 8:22-25
k. Mark 10:13-16

6. At the core of Christian theology is the notion of incarnation—that God became fully present in a human body. What might the theology of incarnation have to say to a theology of the female body? How does incarnation suggest a valuing of human bodies? Many theologians note that incarnation is a continuing process—God is still incarnated in each person. What might this suggest for a theology of the female body?

7. Many feminist theologians would argue that misogyny (hatred of women) is a primary sin of patriarchy, and one of its expressions is the devaluing and harming of the female body—through domestic violence, sexual assault, sexual abuse, the dieting industry, pornography, prostitution and sex trafficking, the fashion industry, and control of women's reproductive functions. If these are sins against women, what would redemption look like? What would be the church's role in redemption? How would redemption be different for men and women?

8. Throughout history, patriarchal institutions have used women's bodies as an excuse to exclude women from power. In some cultures, women were isolated during their menstrual periods and considered unclean. The Catholic Church excludes women from the priesthood because, the Church argues, Jesus was a man, and so a woman cannot possibly represent Jesus because she has the wrong kind of body. What other social and cultural practices can you identify that use women's bodies as an excuse to subordinate or exclude women? How might social and cultural practices change if women's bodies were valued equally as God's creations?

9. Imagine a world of equality for men and women, for people of color and white people, for people with disabilities and people who are able-bodied, for fat people and thin people. How would bodies be viewed in such a world? How would this world be shaped to accommodate all kinds of bodies?

10. Process theology contends that the goal of all entities is enjoyment—being fully present and attentive to each moment, being fully alive in one's present experience. Sin is what prevents enjoyment. Within this framework, how is the devaluing of female bodies sin? What would true enjoyment look like for people with female bodies?

11. How do you feel now that you've thought about female bodies in this way? Can you used what you've learned to feel better about your own body? What can you do to challenge the ways culture makes women feel about their bodies?

Write a thank you note to your body. Express your love and concern for your own body. Offer a prayer of thanksgiving to God for your body.

Exercise 48

A Usable Christian Past

Feminists developed the notion of a usable past as a way to recognize that, despite the long history of misogyny and oppression, alternative traditions and ways of thinking have always challenged sexism and provided egalitarian models for Christian relations. These alternative views can help point us toward the future by providing us with hope, examples, and understandings to challenge the oppressions of our own time.

1. God's Mission

We can begin our quest for a usable past by thinking about God's mission in the world. What is our understanding of why God created the world and how God acts in the world? Where do women fit into God's mission? Does God's mission include women's equality? What is your evidence?

2. The Biblical Prophets

The prophets have a great deal to say about justice. Read the following passages: Isaiah 1:12-17; 10:1-4; 58:6-7; 61:1-3; Jeremiah 7:1-7; 22:3-5; Amos 5:10-15, 21-15; Micah 6:6-8; Zechariah 7:8-10; Malachi 3:1-6.

Questions

1. What do you think these passages say about the oppression of women?

2. How might they challenge traditions that cast women as subordinate or of less value than men?

3. What would they say to contemporary issues such as domestic violence, the feminization of poverty, sexual abuse and sexual assault, workplace harassment, the wage gap between women and men, the exclusion of women from leadership, and the depiction of women as objects for male pleasure?

In the tradition of the prophets, write a modern-day prophetic statement about one of these issues.

3. Jesus

How did Jesus relate to women? Turn to the stories of Mary and Martha (Luke 1:38-42; John 11:1-45; 12:1-7), the Samaritan woman at the well (John 4:4-39), Mary Magdalene (Luke 8:1-3; Matt 27:51–28:10; Mark 16:1-11; John 20:1-18), the hemorrhaging woman (Matt 9:20-22; Mark 5:24-34; Luke 8:43-48), the woman who anointed Jesus (Matt 26:6-13; Mark 14:3-9); the woman who bathed Jesus' feet with her tears (Luke 7:36-50), and the woman caught in adultery (John 8:1-11).

Questions

1. During the time of Jesus, women had few rights; they were essentially the property of men. How did Jesus treat them? What value did he place on women?

2. If Jesus were the model for the treatment of women, what would this mean for women's status today?

3. How do the stories of Jesus challenge the exclusion and oppression of women?

4. Movements Outside the Mainstream

While traditional Christianity developed in such a way that women were excluded from leadership and relegated to submissive roles, some groups saw things differently. Typically, the roles of women seemed to open up during the more radical early days of these groups, and the new openness often fell back into more traditional patriarchal hierarchies once the group was established. Some groups were more progressive on women's rights in some areas than others. Nonetheless, these groups provide historical examples of times when women were treated more equally.

How might attempts by these groups at more egalitarian practices help provide us with a usable Christian past? Investigate these groups to find out how they understood the nature and place of women. Have they maintained egalitarian practices? If so, how did they do this? If not, what happened? What can we learn from the histories of these groups?

- Quakers
- Shakers
- Separate Baptists
- The Four Square Church
- Anabaptists
- Pentecostals
- Seventh Day Adventists

5. Herstory

One of the most important things we can do to create a usable Christian past for women is to reclaim women's stories, to learn "herstory." Choose several of the women below (or divide the list among the members of your group) to research online or at the library.

- Blandina
- Perpetua and Felicitas
- Clare of Assisi
- Brigit of Kildare
- Hildegard of Bingen
- Julian of Norwich
- Catherine of Siena
- Teresa of Avila
- Thérèse de Lisieux
- Olga of Kiev
- Jeanne Jugan
- Katharine Zell
- Mary MacKillop
- Sarah and Angelina Grimké
- Martha Stearns Marshall
- Anne Dutton
- Elizabeth Ann Seton
- Edith Stein
- Aimee Semple McPherson
- Pandita Ramabai
- Anna Howard Shaw
- Lucy Farrow
- Cornelia Jones Robertson
- Dorothy Day
- Evangeline Booth
- Phoebe Palmer
- Joan of Arc

Questions

1. What do these women's stories teach us that can help us create a more just and equitable world for women?

2. How do their stories challenge social and religious barriers to women's full participation in society?

3. What do their stories teach us about the intersections of gender with race/ethnicity, nation, and social class? How does your story fit into herstory?

Exercise 49

Your Church's History

Has anyone written a recent history of your local church? Maybe now's the time for you to try your hand as a church historian.

Begin by combing your church's archives and library. You'll want to gather statistical data, earlier histories, minutes of meetings, letters, bulletins, newsletters, publicity materials, directories, journals, photographs, and whatever other artifacts are on hand to tell the story of your congregation. You should also check with your local association or conference or synod to see what information they have about your church. Additionally, visit your local library or go online to find references to your church in news articles through the years. You can even conduct oral histories with long-time members of the congregation to uncover their stories and memories.

Here are some guiding questions as you examine the artifacts you've collected:

- What's the story of your church's founding? Why was it founded? What were the historical, social, political, economic, and religious circumstances surrounding its founding? How were women involved in its founding?
- How is the beginning of your church located in a larger denominational history or in nondenominational history?
- Who was involved in the founding? What was their agenda? What were their circumstances?
- Who formed the leadership? Why those individuals? What about those not in leadership? What was their role?
- How did the church continue? Was there growth? Who were subsequent leaders? Were there controversies?
- Have there been divisions and splits?
- Have there been successful enterprises or dismal failures?
- Are there connections between your church's ongoing story and your denomination's?
- How is your church's story connected to the larger story of the entire Christian church?
- How did your church respond to important historical events, such as the Civil War, women's suffrage, the civil rights movement, or the women's movement?
- Where have women been involved? In particular, pay attention to the importance of women's often unheralded contributions in service.
- How has power operated in your church's history? Who has had power, and who hasn't? How has power been used well? How has it been abused? What have been the power relations between women and men?
- What major changes have happened in your church? Perhaps these have been theological or administrative. Perhaps your church had to move to another neighborhood or rebuild after a flood.

- What has your church contributed to the life of your community through the years? Who has been most involved?
- What has been the role of children and youth in your congregation? How has this evolved over time?
- Has your church paid attention to disabilities? Has it provided sign language interpretation or Braille texts or easy-to-access ramps?
- Whom has your church included? Whom has it excluded?
- How is your social location affecting your interpretation of your church's story?

As you think about organizing the story of your church, you may consider telling a chronological tale—this happened between 1850 and 1900, and this happened between 1900 and 1950. You may also want to consider telling the story thematically: organization, leadership, controversies, buildings, etc.

Think about how you want to present your history. Do you want to provide a bound manuscript for the church library? Perhaps you can develop a narrated slide show that can be presented during a worship service. Maybe you want to create a YouTube video or use social media to tell the story.

Telling your church's history isn't just a matter of repeating facts about the church. Your task is to interpret those facts in a good story that tells your readers something important about your church and about what it means to be a community of faith. Don't forget to ask the hard questions, answer them honestly and thoughtfully, and point the way toward an even better future.

Exercise 50

The Question of Women's Ordination

Christians often disagree over theological perspectives. Understanding the wide spectrum of arguments and the impact of these perspectives can help you reach your own conclusions about controversial issues. This exercise will help you examine the arguments for and against women's ordination.

Reasons Women Should Not Be Ordained

The Bible says so.

Adam was created first, then Eve.

Eve was first in the Fall.

Gender roles are ordained by God.

Women are to be in submission to men.

All the apostles were male.

Traditionally, the church has only ordained men.

Christ was a man, and so only a man can represent Christ.

Women can serve in a multitude of other ways.

Reasons Women Should Be Ordained

Women are gifted to preach and pastor.

Women are called by God.

Women and men are created equal.

The Bible says that in Christ there is neither male nor female.

Jesus called women to follow him, and women were the first to proclaim the resurrection.

Women served as deacons and apostles in the early church.

Ordination is not a biblical practice, so the Bible does not preclude it.

The passages about women keeping silent and being submissive do not apply.

Women in ministry meet needs in the church.

Questions

1. What is your understanding of ordination?

2. Why is ordination important? Or why not? Is it necessary for pastoral ministry or administration of the sacraments/ordinances?

3. Why is the ordination of women such a controversial topic?

4. How would you assess the arguments above for and against women's ordination?

5. What do churches that prohibit women's ordination stand to lose if women are ordained? What do they lose if women are not ordained?

6. What do churches that ordain women stand to lose if women are not ordained?

7. Some churches that prohibit women from holding positions as pastors make the argument that women should not hold authority over men. What does this argument suggest that these churches understand about the role of the pastor? Do you think the role of the pastor is one of authority over the congregation? What are other models of pastoral leadership?

8. The Catholic Church argues that Jesus' maleness was not incidental and therefore for a priest to represent Christ, he must be male like Jesus. Do you think the maleness of Jesus was essential to his role and function as the incarnation of God? Do you think the priest or pastor must share the same physical attributes as Jesus in order to represent God to the congregation?

9. Women who seek ordination explain that they are called by God to preach and pastor. Those who oppose women's ordination say that these women are wrong and have misheard the call of God. Is it appropriate for Christian leaders to decide who and who has not been called by God? Can someone else know if an individual has or has not been called? What should a woman do if she feels called by God to ordained ministry but her church/denomination does not ordain women?

10. What might ordained women bring to ministry that could benefit the church?

Exercise 51

Religion in a Liberal Democracy

Freedom of religion and the separation of church and state are cornerstones of American democracy. Nonetheless, our religious selves and political selves are not separate entities, and so we bring our religious convictions to the public square. In a pluralistic democracy such as ours, conflicts inevitably arise because of our various perspectives. In these contentious issues we have to look to find a balance between allowing people their perspectives and protecting the civil and human rights of all. The following exercise examines your knowledge of religious liberty in the US and encourages you to think about how we apply the First Amendment in public policy.

Religious Liberty Quiz

1. Name the five freedoms in the 1st Amendment.

2. In what instances can government regulate speech?

3. What two clauses of the 1st Amendment deal with religious liberty?

4. What does the 1st Amendment say about religion?

5. What is the only mention of religion in the text of the Constitution (not including the Bill of Rights)?

6. What was the first colony founded on the basis of religious liberty?

7. Who founded that colony?

8. In what document does Thomas Jefferson refer to the "wall of separation" between church and state?

9. What religious group agitated for the 1st Amendment?

10. Who threatened to run against James Madison for the Constitutional Convention if Madison would not support a bill of rights that included religious liberty?

11. In what state did this happen?

12. What religion were George Washington and Thomas Jefferson?

13. What must the government demonstrate to interfere in religion?

14. What are some examples?

15. What must employers provide for religious employees?

16. What practices can employers not require if people have religious objections?

17. What can employees do if they have religious objections to paying union dues?

18. Why have courts ruled that creationism and intelligent design cannot be taught in public schools?

19. What three criteria must be used to assess legislation regarding religion (the Lemon test)?

20. Which of the following practices have been ruled by the US Supreme Court to be unconstitutional?
   a. school-initiated prayer in a public school

   b. using school loudspeakers to offer a student-led, student-initiated prayer

   c. requirement that Jehovah's Witnesses say the Pledge of Allegiance and salute the American flag

   d. devotional Bible reading in public school classroom

   e. prohibition of teaching evolution in public schools

   f. court interference in matters of church doctrine, discipline, or polity

   g. disqualification of clergy from public office

   h. posting the Ten Commandments in public school classroom

   i. restrictions on religious groups meeting in state university buildings

   j. requirement of moment of silence or meditation in public schools

   k. clergy offering prayer during public school graduation

l. granting churches veto power over nearby issuance of liquor licenses

m. state requirement to display state motto on vehicle license plates that violates owner's religious convictions

n. requiring attendance at public schools

o. allowing clerics to hold religious classes at public schools during school hours

(Answers appear at the end of the workbook.)

Separation of church and state and freedom of religion are two of the founding principles of American liberal democracy. According to Thomas Jefferson, religion should have no influence on a citizen's civil rights. Religious difference has been preserved within a symbolically homogenous shared value system centered on citizenship, but certain religious groups have at various times been considered outside accepted norms of deviation (early Mormons, for example). Some deeply religious people may feel forced to deny a major part of their identity within the public realm.

What happens when religious convictions come into conflict with citizenship in a pluralistic society? Think about the following controversial topics that have a legal or public policy aspect. What are varying religious views on the topic? On its legal/policy status? How can the state both honor individuals' religious convictions and recognize each citizen's legal rights?

- Abortion
- Same-sex marriage
- Right to die (physician-assisted suicide)
- Fetal stem cell research
- Health insurance coverage for contraceptives

Exercise 52

What's Your Church's Position? What's Yours?

This exercise will require you to do a little research. You may want to use your web search engine, your church library, and members of your church/denomination to help find the answers. Below are a number of important topics for women and the contemporary church. Find out what your church or denomination's stance on the issue is. Summarize that stance in the second column. Then, in the third column, briefly write your stance on the issue. You may want to read a number of Christian theologians and ethicists on the issue to inform your answer.

The Issue	**Your Church or Denomination's Stance**	**Your Stance**
Assisted Reproductive Technologies (such as in-vitro fertilization and surrogacy)		
Birth Control		
Abortion		
Deliberate Childlessness		
Same-sex Relationships		
Same-sex Marriage		
Wifely Submission		
Divorce		
Homeschooling		
Women's Work Outside the Home		
Ordination of Women		
Women Pastors		

1. Go back through the chart and highlight any stances that you believe are empowering to women. Explain your reasoning.

2. Now highlight any stances that you believe are disempowering for women. Explain your reasoning.

3. Overall, how would you assess the place of women in the contemporary church? How would you assess the church's contribution to the lives of women?

4. Identify other contemporary issues that are of concern to women.

5. What are your church's and your stances on these issues?

6. If you found that your beliefs are in conflict with your church's, what were the differences? How important are those differences to you?

7. If you were uncertain about your own beliefs regarding some of these issues, where did you turn for information? What information did you consider authoritative? What information did you reject? How did you determine which sources were reliable and which were not trustworthy?

8. What did you learn from this activity about examining contemporary issues for women in light of church stances and other information? How might this activity influence your examination of other issues in the future?

Exercise 53

What's in Your Backpack?

We all carry our histories and our social locations into every interaction. Feminist Peggy McIntosh calls a part of what we carry "privilege" (Peggy McIntosh, "White Privilege and Male Privilege: Unpacking the Invisible Knapsack," *Peace and Freedom* [July/August 1989]: 10–12). By *privilege*, she means "an invisible package of unearned assets." She uses white privilege as an example. She says that simply by being white, she receives a number of advantages. For example, she explains, she can go shopping in a nice department store and not be followed by store employees because of her race. Mostly, we don't have to be aware of our privilege (that's part of the privilege), and yet our privilege affects everything we do, including how we do theology.

This exercise asks you to think about your privilege. Privilege accrues to the dominant social categories in a culture. Below are a number of dominant statuses in the US. Using McIntosh's example, make a list of ways you have privilege in the categories that apply to you. A few other examples are offered below.

WHITE
I can go to a bank for a loan and be sure that my race won't work against me.

MALE
If I have both children and a career, no one will think I am a bad parent for working.

ADULT (but not elderly)
People don't assume that I'm hard of hearing and raise their voices to talk to me.

ABLE-BODIED
I can go into any building and assume that I can navigate it easily to find my intended destination.

CHRISTIAN
My religious holidays are embedded in the social and work calendar.

Questions

1. Take a look at your lists. Now think about your church. How do you see privilege embedded in your church?

2. How do you think privilege affects how you read the Bible or do theology or think about ethical issues?

3. How can your awareness of privilege help you be open to other perspectives?

Doing Ecotheology

We live in a time of environmental crisis, from climate change and global warming to pollution to the loss of plant and animal species. For some Christians, the environment is not an important issue. Either they see the natural world as something to be dominated because of their interpretation of the command in Genesis to subdue the earth, or they see it as irrelevant because the focus of the Christian is on the world to come, not this one. Some may even see environmental destruction as an inevitable precursor to an apocalypse. Other Christians, however, believe that a close connection exists between Christian theology and the natural world. They may see the created world as a good gift from God given to humans as its stewards, or they may see humans as yet another facet of God's good creation who are in intimate relationship with the world of which they are a part.

How can we construct a theology of the environment? Take the following steps to build your own ecotheology.

1. Explore the tradition. A number of Christian thinkers across the ages have demonstrated a keen awareness of the importance of the natural world (such as Hildegard of Bingen or Francis of Assisi).

2. Think about traditional theological themes in terms of the environment. How would we reshape these themes to take the natural world into account?

a. Incarnation

b. The Spirit

c. Creation

d. Human nature

e. Redemption

f. Worship

g. Eschatology

h. Justice

3. Imagine a meeting of a reflective Christian, an ecofeminist, a scientist, an anthropologist, a philosopher, a Buddhist, and a Jew. What would each of these perspectives bring to the table? Do some research on the views of these groups. How can they inform your own ecotheology?

4. Experience the sacred in the natural world. Go for a hike, relax by a lake, walk barefoot on the sand, lie on your back and gaze at the stars. What do you learn from direct experience in nature? How do you experience God in nature?

5. What would it mean to develop an earth-centered theology? In this approach, the earth is central because no human or animal life we know can exist without it. This makes the earth our starting point in doing theology. What would an earth-centered theology say about the relationship between humans and the earth? How would it emphasize the sacredness of the earth? How would it envision how humans treat the earth? How would it see the encounter between humans and God mediated by the earth? How would it understand gender? How would it define sin and redemption? How would it connect with social justice? How would it envision a hopeful utopian future?

6. What do you think? How do you understand the environment and its connection to faith?

See Heather Eaton, *Introducing Ecofeminist Theologies* (London: T & T Clark International, 2005).

Exercise 55

Applying Tools for Ethical Decision-making

We are often faced with difficult ethical decisions. The modern world has brought with all its advances even more tricky situations as we contemplate the role of technology and globalization. More and more we find ourselves facing situations that may not have clear-cut answers. This exercise will help you apply the five questions of ethics to a dilemma and to imagine how these questions might help you deal with ethical questions in your own life.

Choose one of the following ethical dilemmas or divide the dilemmas among your group members. Apply the questions below and determine options for an ethical decision.

Dilemmas

- Doctors have pronounced a family member brain dead. You must make the decision whether or not to terminate life support.
- A close friend has received the news that her fetus is severely deformed. Her doctors have suggested an abortion. She has come to you for advice.
- A local organization is soliciting donations to help with disaster relief for a nearby town. While you find this cause worthy, you also know that this organization holds a number of positions that differ from your own.
- You have been offered funding to conduct a project that will help address hunger in your area, but the funder is a corporation that pollutes the environment.
- You watch your money closely and try to be a thrifty shopper. A new store has opened in town that has low prices, but it also has a history of poor working conditions and discrimination against women and people of color.
- Your church houses a program for HIV prevention. The program would like to begin a needle exchange. The congregation has to vote on the issue.
- You are on the local school board. A group of concerned parents has proposed a sex education curriculum for a local middle school.
- You are a juror on a first-degree murder case. The defendant has been convicted and now the prosecutor has asked the jury to recommend the death penalty.
- You are a schoolteacher. A student has come to you and told you that he is being bullied because he is gay.
- Your local power company is giving customers the option to sign up for clean energy (such as wind power). The clean energy costs a little more, but it puts fewer pollutants into the environment.

• A high school girl in your Sunday school class tells you that she has been sexually assaulted by the star football player who also attends your church.
• Your retirement advisor tells you about a rapidly growing company with strong returns on investment and advises you to invest right away. The company's profits are closely related to its use of laborers in other countries who often work in dangerous conditions and in sweatshops.

Questions

1. What is the most loving thing I can do in this situation?

2. How tender can I bear to be?

3. Am I in right relationship with all those involved?

4. What if everyone behaved like me? Would the world be a better place?

5. How do I include myself in the circle of those for whom I offer love and care?

What feelings were evoked as you reflected on the ethical dilemma you selected? Have you ever faced a similar dilemma? What happened then and how did you feel about it? How do you feel in situations in which the right thing to do is not clear and unambiguous? Can you describe a time when you were in such a situation? What did you do? How did you make your decisions?

Are there ethical dilemmas you are facing right now? What might your answers to the five questions above have to say to those issues?

Exercise 56

Walking without a Camera

Annie Dillard writes about our need to be attentive to the world around us. She says that the difference between two ways of seeing is the difference between walking with and without a camera. When she walks with a camera, she walks from shot to shot. When she walks without a camera, her own shutter opens up and records the moment onto her being (Annie Dillard, *Pilgrim at Tinker Creek* [New York: Bantam, 1974] 33). Spirituality calls us to walk without a camera, to pay attention to the wonders all around us, to find God in every place and moment.

We can begin to learn to walk without a camera by getting in touch with our own bodies. Imagine that you are in a race, but the goal is to be the slowest. Now, as slowly as possible, race across the room. As you do, pay attention to your body, to your muscles, to your movement. What do you notice? Now make yourself as small as possible. Then make yourself as big as possible. What do you notice? The Bible tells us that we are fearfully and wonderfully made. What do you notice about the wonder of your own body?

Take an apple or an orange or a piece of chocolate and spend three minutes sensing it. Look at it closely. Sketch it. Describe it with words. Touch it. What does it feel like? Smell it. How would you describe the smell? Taste it. How would you describe the taste? How can you experience the presence of God in everyday things like fruit or chocolate? Taste and see that the Lord is good, the Bible tells us.

Take a walk outside. Walk slowly and pay attention to the world around you. Look at it, touch it, smell it, hear it. When you come back, write about your experience. Think about how you experience God in the world around you.

Drawing on your sensory experience, list a few of your favorite things:

Seeing

Tasting

Touching

Hearing

Smelling

Matthew Fox, an Episcopalian priest and theologian, says that these deep, joyful experiences are experiences of God (*Whee! We, Wee All the Way Home: A Guide to Sensual Prophetic Spirituality* [Rochester

VT: Bear & Company, 1980]). When we pay attention to our experiences, we can develop a heightened awareness of God's presence and be prepared for authentic encounters with God. In these moments we become fully alive, fully attentive to joy, wonder, and mystery.

Learning to see God's presence all around us is both a discipline and a gift. Certainly, God's presence sometimes pushes its way into our consciousness. But we must also develop the discipline of looking for it in unexpected places. We may expect to find God in church, but do we also look for God on the freeway or at a football game or on a beach? Think about the places where you experience God's presence. What can you do to become more attentive to the ongoing presence of God in your daily activities? We are always standing on holy ground, but we must prepare ourselves to see it.

Exercise 57

Traveling Tips

While you are coming to the end of this book and workbook, you are still on your way in your journey as a reflective Christian. Imagine where you want to go from here.

1. How do you imagine yourself being open to new experiences and ideas? How can you use what you've learned to help your process along the way?

2. How do you imagine yourself learning from those who are different from yourself? When and where do you encounter people who are different from you? Do you seek out opportunities to meet different people and hear different perspectives? How might these opportunities enhance your faith journey?

3. How do you handle things when you encounter unexpected bumps in the road? How comfortable are you with not knowing? What can you learn from those moments when you are unsure or end up somewhere other than the place you intended?

4. What brings you joy? How do you understand the role of joy in your faith journey? How do you express gratitude for your experiences of joy?

5. Who travels on your faith journey with you? Who helps you grapple with questions and celebrate breakthroughs? Whose shoulder do you cry on and who cries on yours? How do you support each other on your faith journey?

6. What have you learned about loving God with your mind? How do you understand what it means to be a reflective Christian?

7. What will you carry with you from this part of the journey?

Selected Answers

Exercise 5, The Authoritative Text, p. 10
The correct version is the New York Manuscript version.

I think nothing is religion which puts one individual absolutely above others, and surely nothing is religion which puts one sex above another. Religion is primarily our relation to the Supreme, to God himself. It is for him to judge; it is for him to say where we belong, who is highest and who is not; of that we know nothing. And any religion which will sacrifice a certain set of human beings for the enjoyment or aggrandizement or advantage of another is no religion. It is a thing which may be allowed, but it is against true religion. Any religion which sacrifices women to the brutality of men is no religion.

Exercise 9, Identifying Sources III, p. 18

(1) E; (2) P; (3) J; (4) P; (5) D; (6) P; (7) J; (8) Likely J and E blended; (9) P; (10) D.

Exercise 51: Religious Liberty Quiz, p. 138

1. religion, speech, press, assembly, petition
2. fighting words, national security
3. establishment, free exercise
4. "Congress shall make no law respecting an establishment of religion or prohibiting the free exercise thereof."
5. no religious test for public office
6. Rhode Island
7. Roger Williams
8. letter to the Baptists of Danbury, Connecticut
9. Baptists
10. John Leland
11. Virginia
12. Deist
13. compelling interest
14. medical treatment for the children of Christian Scientists, blood transfusions for the children of Jehovah's Witnesses, use of peyote by Native Americans
15. reasonable accommodation
16. yoga, meditation, New Age practices
17. equal donation to charity
18. religious intent
19. First, the statute must have a secular legislative purpose; second, its principal or primary effect must be one that neither advances nor inhibits religion; third, the statute must not foster an excessive government entanglement with religion.
20. All have been found unconstitutional.

16974795R00094

Made in the USA
San Bernardino, CA
25 November 2014